FAITH PAPERS

Vic Reasoner

Fundamental

fWP

WESLEYAN
PUBLISHERS

2120 Culverson Ave
Evansville, IN 47714-4811

Table of Contents

FAITH PAPERS

First Paper. Faith Defined

If we cannot please God without faith and if we are saved by faith alone, and if the just are to live by that same faith, we can expect the devil to bring confusion about faith. Much of the popular teaching about faith is fuzzy.

- Is faith an irrational leap?
- Is it accepting certain doctrinal truths?
- Is it a sincere wish?
- Is it pretending as hard as you can even when you don't understand?
- Is it presumption or a presupposition?
- Is it an innate ability which we choose to exercise or release?
- Is faith the belief in the power of positive thinking?

The Greek word for *faith* is πίστις (*pistis*). It carries the ideas of belief, trust, confidence, and fidelity. It comes from the verb πείθω (*peitho*) which means to be persuaded. The verb form of *pistis* is πιστεύω (*pisteuo*) which means to entrust.

Ralph Winter distinguished between the noun and the verb.

Faith, then, is not something we conjure nor work up, nor is it mere courage, it is the gift of God, something totally God's initiative. . . . Believing, on the other hand, is a verb, not a noun. *Belief* refers to what we do, not what God gives. *Faith* is what God gives. *Faith* is what we believe IN. Belief is our response to faith; it is walking in the heaven-given light of faith; walking in faith. . . . Believing, then, is not merely an intellectual but also a volitional response to faith. It is obedience: true heart obedience.[1]

Biblical faith is essentially trust in God. We cannot separate who he is from what he has said. His name and his word are exalted above all things (Ps 138:2).

Everyone believes something. Atheism and agnosticism are both faith claims. Saving faith requires the transfer of trust in ourselves to trust in God. Such faith is necessary in order to please God (Heb 11:6). According to Hebrews 11:1, faith is both a divine persuasion and a divine confidence.

This persuasion is based upon evidence and is not a leap of presumption. William Lane translated this opening phrase, "Now faith celebrates the objective reality of the blessings for which we hope."[2] "It is that full assent unto truths credible upon the testimony of God."[3]

Martin Luther declared, "Faith is a living, daring confidence in God's grace, so sure and certain that the believer

---

[1]Winter, "Theology of Redemption," 15.

[2]Lane, W*BC*, 47B:325.

[3]Binney and Steele, *TPC*, 616.

would stake his life on it a thousand times."[4]

John Wesley wrote,

> Christian faith is then not only an assent to the whole gospel of Christ, but also a full reliance on the blood of Christ, a trust in the merits of his life, death, and resurrection; a recumbency upon him as our atonement and our life, *as given for us*, and *living in us*. It is a sure confidence which a man hath in God, that through the merits of Christ *his* sins are forgiven, and *he* reconciled to the favor of God.[5]

Daniel Steele explained,

> Saving faith is not a leap in the dark, as some teach, but a firm stepping upon God's recorded willingness and ability to grant present deliverance from the guilt of sin, til we step upon the last stone which is the Spirit's testimony — "He doeth it."[6]

Everyone does not have faith (2 Thess 3:2). Faith is not simply a natural ability which we choose to exercise. Saving faith has three components.

- ***Faith is based on intellectual persuasion.***

The Bible refers to "the faith" in instances such as

---

[4]Luther, *Luther's Works*, 35:370-371.

[5]Wesley, "Salvation by Faith," Sermon #1, 1.5.

[6]Steele, *Half-Hours with St. Paul*, 316; quoted by Smith, *Jesus Lifting Chinese*, 124.

Galatians 1:23, Ephesians 4:5, 13, Philippians 1:27, 1 Timothy 4:1, 2 Peter 2:1, and Jude 3. "The faith" refers to the collective beliefs which the church held in common. They were handed down by the apostles and are non-negotiable. Yet it is possible to intellectually affirm "the faith" and not have saving faith personally.

God has sufficiently revealed himself to all mankind (Rom 1:19-23). All attempts to disprove God are self defeating.

- Atheism allows that we exist, but our existence is contingent on an uncaused cause which they deny. I don't have enough faith to be an atheist! Why do atheists spend their time attempting to refute something that does not exist? The real question is not *whether* God is, but *who* God is. "The only atheism that the Scripture admits is practical atheism."[7] According to Psalm 14:1, "the fool has said in his heart, 'There is no God.'" The Hebrew word נבל (*nabal*), translated *fool*, describes this insensitivity to ethical and spiritual claims.

- Agnosticism asserts that we can know nothing absolutely for sure about God. But are you sure about that? How can an agnostic be sure of his doubts? In order to doubt anything, one must know something — otherwise one would not even know what he is doubting. We do not know everything about God, yet there is *sufficient* reason to believe in God.

- Pantheism reduces everything to a single essence. It holds that God exists, but I do not exist. I am simply part

---

[7]Pope, *Compendium*, 1:235.

of the divine. C. S. Lewis explained,

> Once, before creation, it would have been true to say that everything was God. But God created: He caused things to be other than Himself that, being distinct, they might learn to love Him, and achieve union instead of mere sameness.[8]

In other words, there must be a distinction between the creator and the creation (Heb 11:3).

• Postmodernism says there is no overarching truth — which is itself quite a sweeping truth claim! Everyone has his own story, his own reality. Ultimate reality is unknowable, only your perspective. If everyone has his own reality, the result is a world of isolation. The result is a God-sized vacuum.

If there is sufficient evidence for God, the problem lies within us. No one is born an atheist. Many skeptics and infidels have had a conservative religion background. They have chosen *not* to believe because they were unwilling to accept the consequences of that faith. Thus, having rejected truth, they were abandoned to intellectual darkness.

Faith is reasonable. Yet saving faith must go beyond intellectual persuasion.

• ***Faith involves a consent of our will.***

Faith always contains action. It is not simply being convinced intellectually. People often tell the pastor, "I believe,

---

[8]Lewis, *The Problem of Pain*, 150-151.

I'm just not living right." That level faith will not save them. This is the faith of demons (Jas 2:19). Over 100 million Americans think they are going to heaven because they have repeated a salvation prayer.[9] Yet 90% of those who have prayed such a prayer show no fruit of salvation.[10] True faith always produces action. This obedience of faith is referenced in Romans 1:5 and 16:26. In Romans 2:13-29, 9:30-32, and 10:16 Paul also equates obedience with faith.

True faith involves both an initial submission and continued obedience. Douglas Moo wrote, "Obedience always involves faith, and faith always involves obedience. They should not be equated, compartmentalized, or made into separate stages of Christian experience."[11]

Moo echoed Dietrich Bonhoeffer who wrote, "Only he who believes is obedient and only he who is obedient believes."[12] Daniel Steele also taught that the obedience of faith for the sinner is repentance and for the believer it is to keep the commandments of Christ.[13]

In Hebrews 3:18 the KJV says "believed not." The NIV says "disobeyed." Which is it — *disbelieved* or *disobeyed*? Actually it is both. The Greek word ἀπειθέω (*apeitheo*) means that they refused to be persuaded. The conclusion in v 19 equates this disobedience with unbelief (ἀπιστία - *apistia*). Disobedience is the result of unbelief.

---

[9]McIntyre, *The Graham Formula*, 107, 44-53.

[10]Comfort and Cameron, *The School Of Biblical Evangelism,* 133.

[11]Moo, *Romans 1-8*, 44-45.

[12]Bonhoffer, *The Cost of Discipleship*, 69.

[13]Steele, *Milestone Papers*, 73-77.

Faith is of the heart, invisible to men; obedience is of the conduct and may be observed. When a man obeys God he gives the only possible evidence that in his heart he believes God. Of course it is persuasion of the truth that results in faith (we believe because we are persuaded that the thing is true, a thing does not become true because it is believed).[14]

The Greek verb πείθω (*peitho*) means to be persuaded and is closely related to *pisteuo*, the word for *believe*. *Peitho* is translated *trust* or *believe* in Matthew 27:43, Mark 10:24, Luke 11:22, 18:9, Acts 17:4, 27:11, 28:24, 2 Corinthians 1:9, 10:7, Philippians 2:24, 3:4, Hebrews 2:13, 13:18. It is translated *obey* in Acts 5:36-37, Romans 2:8, Galatians 3:1, 5:7, Hebrews 13:17, and James 3:3.

Therefore, we must trust *and* obey. Faith and obedience are two sides of the same coin. Since the supreme disobedience is a refusal to believe the gospel, the meaning of *apeitheo* may mean disbelieve and thus may describe an unbeliever in some contexts.[15] This illustrates the close connection between faith and obedience. Clarke wrote, "Unbelief and disobedience are so intimately connected, that the same word in the sacred writings often serves for *both*."[16] In John 3:36, Jesus declared that whoever *believes* has eternal life; whoever *does not obey* shall not see life.

Saving faith is not given until we have repented. God commands all people everywhere to repent (Acts 17:30). Foster explained, "An impenitent soul cannot exercise faith."

---

[14]Vine, *Expository Dictionary*, 3:124.

[15]Arndt and Gingrich, *Lexicon*, 82.

[16]Clarke, *Commentary*, 5:358.

We cannot commit ourselves to God while at the same time we are in rebellion against God.[17] If we will repent, God will give us faith (Eph 2:8; Phil 1:29). God will show us that he is real, that his Word is true, that Christ is the only way of salvation, and that he has forgiven and accepted us. This assurance is the operation of the Holy Spirit. Therefore, faith always contains strong assurance.

But God will not exercise faith for us. Adam Clarke wrote,

> Is not *faith* the *gift of God*? Yes, as to the *grace*, by which it is produced; but the *grace* or *power* to believe, and the *act* of *believing*, are two different things. Without the *grace* or *power* to believe no man ever did or can believe; but with that *power* the *act* of *faith* is a man's own. God never believes *for* any man, no more than he *repents* for him; the penitent, through this grace enabling him, believes for him: nor does he believe *necessarily*, or *impulsively* when he has that power; the power to believe may be present long before it is exercised, else, why the solemn warnings with which we meet every where in the word of God, and threatenings against those who do not believe? Is not this a proof that such persons have the *power* but do not use it? *They believe not*, and therefore *are not established*. This, therefore, is the true state of the case: God gives the power, man uses the power thus given, and brings glory to God: without the power no man can believe;

---

[17]Foster, *Philosophy of Christian Experience*, 103-104.

with it, any man may.[18]

Thus, faith is our response to God's revelation (Rom 10:17). It is being convinced in our mind, the consent of our will, and receiving divine confirmation. S. A. Keen was representative of American holiness teaching and was in error when he wrote,

> Saving faith is not the gift of God in any proper sense. . . . We have the power to believe, and have the Word of God which is to be believed; and when we choose to believe that Word — that *is* faith. Saving faith is *not* a gracious state of the heart wrought by some sovereign power of the Holy Spirit.[19]

Preliminary grace is that window of opportunity in which God enables us to believe. At some point in time and to some degree, every person is awakened. If we respond to this drawing grace, it will increase. Wesley said the generality of men stifle it as soon as possible and after a while forget or at least deny that ever they had it at all.[20]

• ***Faith produces divine assurance.***

While faith is rational and does not bypass our mind, faith always contains an unknown element. We cannot discover God through the pursuit of philosophy alone. God must

---

[18]Clarke, *Commentary*, 6:439, 1069. See also Wesley, *Letter* to Theophilus Lessey, 7 Jan 1787.

[19]Keen, *Faith Papers*, 31.

[20]Wesley, "Scripture Way of Salvation," Sermon #43, 1.2.

make himself known to us. He does so at first through his preliminary grace. Those who respond in obedient faith will receive divine assurance.

> The *manner* how the divine testimony is manifested to the heart, I do not take upon me to explain. "Such knowledge is too wonderful and excellent for me; I cannot attain unto it." "The wind bloweth, and I hear the sound thereof;" but I cannot "tell how it cometh, or whither it goeth." As no one knoweth the things of a man, save the spirit of a man that is in him; so the *manner* of the things of God knoweth no one, save the Spirit of God. But the fact we know; namely, that the Spirit of God does give a believer such a testimony of his adoption that while it is present to the soul he can no more doubt the reality of his sonship than he can doubt of the shining of the sun while he stands in the full blaze of his beams.[21]

Wesley also taught

> To this confidence that God is both able and willing to sanctify us *now*, there needs to be added one more thing — a divine evidence and conviction that *he doeth it.*[22]

The assurance of *provision* is an aspect of saving faith. The assurance of *possession* is the witness of the Spirit. Burwash explained,

---

[21]Wesley, "Witness of the Spirit, I," Sermon #10, 1.12.

[22]Wesley, "The Scripture Way of Salvation," Sermon #43, 3.17.

Faith has in it divine assurance, and all assurance springs from God-given faith. Justifying faith is a personal divine assurance of the *provision* of salvation in Christ for me. The witness is personal divine assurance of the *possession* of that salvation in me. Abiding saving faith grows out of and includes the witness, as the justifying act of faith preceded it.[23]

Thus, saving faith is repose. We rest our "weary soul" in God and he gives us the rest of faith (Heb 4:1-11).

---

[23]Burwash, *Wesley's Doctrinal Standards*, 92-93.

Second Paper. The Source of Faith

According to Hebrews 12:2, Jesus is the source — the author, the founder, the originator — of faith. Often, however, faith is expressed in humanistic terms. It is described as potential that we release. Oral Roberts taught that we use our inborn ability to believe and exercise our faith to get well and stay well. However, faith cannot be pumped up emotionally.

The popular notion is that every person has a little spark of God within him. It becomes an irrational leap. However, "not all have faith" (2 Thess 3:2). Scripture teaches that faith is a gift from God.

True faith is not positive thinking. It is not possibility thinking. It is not a positive confession or declaration. When faith is reduced to such concepts, there is little reference to the object of faith. Instead, the emphasis is that faith works. And it seems to work equally well regardless of what we put our faith in! People with faith get through life's problems better. Those in the business world have observed that a positive mental attitude works better than a negative attitude, but anything that is not based in God's Word is presumption, not faith.

Attacks on biblical inerrancy are an attack on faith. According to Romans 10:17-21 faith comes from God. God reveals himself through his Word. If God's Word is not trustworthy, our acceptance of it does not make it so. Paul explained in 1 Corinthians 15:17 that if the resurrection of Christ did not happen, our faith is futile. But if the Word of God is true, it is satanic to deny it. See Genesis 3:1-4.

The passage in Romans 10 explains that those who have not heard the Word have no basis for faith. We must first hear God's Word before we can believe in our hearts. Clearly the basis for true faith, then, is not what *we* declare — despite prosperity teaching — but what God has declared. Thus, our public confession is not faith, but the result of faith.

After we believe, we are then to confess with our mouth that we believe God. It does no good to confess anything that God has not spoken. And it does no good to confess that we are saved if we have not truly believed in our heart. Such belief must include submission. Mary did not understand God's plan, but she declared, "Let it be to me according to your word" (Luke 1:38).

We must accept in order to understand. Jesus promised, "If anyone wants to do his will, he shall know concerning the doctrine, whether it is from God or whether I speak on my own authority" (John 7:17). Commenting on these words, Augustine said, "For understanding is the reward of faith. Therefore do not seek to understand in order to believe, but believe that thou mayest understand."[24] Therefore, faith is the precondition of a proper understanding; submission is necessary before we can receive knowledge.

Mark 11:24 is often misused to teach that if we want something we first confess it and then possess it. Richard Watson gave a classic response.

An ill use has sometimes been made of this passage, as though it meant, that, when praying, whatever we believe, that is, persuade ourselves that we receive, we do receive, — an absurdity and a self-contradic-

[24]Augustine, *Homilies on the Gospels*. Tractate 29 on John 7:14-18. *NPNF*1 7:184.

tion. Here, however, to *believe*, does not signify to persuade ourselves into an opinion; but to trust, or to have faith in God. This trust must necessarily be regulated by God's own PROMISE and WARRANT, and it is exercised IN ORDER that we may receive. The sense therefore is, *believe*, trust, *that ye* shall *receive them*, and *ye shall* obtain *them*; that is, all things which God both expressly promises, and which are, as St. John states, "according to his will."[25]

The fact that Watson wrote this in 1833 indicates that generations have struggled with false conceptions of faith. If we back up to v 22 the statement "have faith in God" states clearly the object of faith. We cannot have faith in God until we accept his revelation.

There are twelve passages which could be translated to say that faith is *of* God or *of* Jesus: Mark 11:22, Romans 3:3, 3:22, 3:26, Galatians 2:16, 2:20, 3:22, 3:26, Ephesians 3:12, Philippians 3:9, Colossians 2:12, Revelation 14:12.

Mark 11:22 reads, "Have faith in God."However, Kenneth Hagin, no Greek scholar, also adopted this objective genitive interpretation for Mark 11:22, which he translates "the God kind of faith." Scholars believe he was influenced by Kenyon or the *Dake Annotated Reference Bible*.[26]

Regardless of his source, his conclusion is that faith

---

[25]Watson, *Exposition*, 380.

[26]E. W. Kenyon also taught God-kind of faith [*Kenyon*, 272-274]. McIntyre includes a section on this passage citing Adam Clarke for support. However, McIntyre is misleading. Clarke explained that "the faith of God" meant strong faith. Wallace explains that the object of our faith is faithfulness [*Greek Grammar*, 116].

becomes an independent power upon which God himself is dependent. Hagin concludes that the "God kind of faith" as evidenced by God in creation is released by words. Hagin writes, "God created the universe with words. Words filled with faith are the most powerful things in all the world."[27] This teaching destroys the omnipotence of God.

But this study also has implications for Calvinism. Romans 3:3 refers to the faithfulness of God as does Philippians 3:9. Colossians 2:12 refers to faith in the powerful work of God. The other eight verses contain both the noun *faith* and the noun *Jesus Christ* in the genitive case. Most of the discussion concerns whether the phrase is an objective genitive, meaning the noun in the genitive *receives* the action or a subjective genitive, when the noun in the genitive *produces* the action. Those who argue for a subjunctive genitive are divided as to whether it means "the faith given by Jesus Christ" or "the faithfulness of Jesus Christ." In 2005 the NET Bible became the first translation to use a subjective genitive translation of Romans 3:22, "through the faithfulness of Jesus Christ."

How should these passages be translated? For example, Romans 3:22 could be translated

- the faith given by Jesus Christ - subjective
- the faithfulness of Jesus Christ - subjective
- faith in Jesus Christ - objective

While there is no doubt that Jesus Christ is the proper object of faith, does the fact that in all twelve instances *faith* is a noun, and not a verb, move away from the idea of human response? Or is the subjective translation trend the result of

---

[27]Hagin, *New Thresholds of Faith*, 74-76.

Calvinistic assumptions?[28]

Galatians 2:16 may be speaking of both aspects of faith within the same verse. The sense of the verse would be — knowing that a man is not justified by works of the law, but by faith in Jesus Christ, even so (καὶ - *kai*) we believed in Christ Jesus, in order that we might be justified [aorist passive subjunctive] by the faithfulness of Christ or faith in Christ. What is clear is that when we believed, we were justified in a single act, since the time action in the subjunctive is relative to that of the main verb. The main teaching of the verse is that in order to be justified we must believe, since no one is justified by observing the law. In either case, believing or observing, there is a human response and two responses are contrasted. One is works; the other is faith. Verse 17 continues by emphasizing our seeking of justification. The point is that faith is clearly an objective human action, even if the last usage in v 16 could have a subjective meaning.

To look at a second passage, Richard Watson takes Romans 3:22 as objective genitive — that our faith is the instrumental cause of justification.

> This justification is, by faith, διὰ πίστεως, διὰ marking the INSTRUMENTAL cause, FAITH; and the object of this faith is *Christ Jesus,* the meritorious or procuring cause of this grace and salvation; for there seems no reason for making a distinction between faith *of* Jesus Christ, and faith *in* Jesus Christ.

But while Romans 3:3 and 3:22 could be interpreted as

---

[28]These assumptions will be explained on p. 26 as "voluntaristic faith."

saying that God was the source of faith, both emphasize the human dimension — our believing. One more passage is worth our consideration. Does Colossians 2:12 say through faith of or in the operation of God?

> Is not faith said to be of the operation of God? No, faith is said to be *in the working* and operation of the God who raised Christ from the dead: it is nowhere declared to be wrought in us directly and independently.[29]

While none of these passages can be used to teach faith is a gift, which passively saves us, yet faith is a gift. Acts 3:16 speaks of "the faith which is by him." In Ephesians 2:8 this "gift of God" probably refers back to the whole process of salvation, which includes grace and faith. According to Hebrews 12:2 he is the author of faith. Yet if the nouns in Galatians 2:16 were interpreted as the gift of faith, we would be justified by the gift of faith from Jesus Christ. However, the same verse makes it clear that we are justified when we believe. We affirm the faith of Jesus Christ as a divine gift and faith in Jesus Christ as a human response.

The doctrinal question is whether the gift of faith is given only to the passive elect as a result of their regeneration or to those who repent and is the basis of their justification. Faith is God-given and God-based, but we must choose to believe him and his Word.

---

[29]Pope, *A Higher Catechism of Theology*, 216.

Third Paper. The Object of Faith

Back in 1888 a holiness evangelist wrote *Faith Papers*, from which I borrowed the title for this book (and little else). He wrote,

> When a boy thirteen years of age, I became deeply convicted of sin, and earnestly anxious to be saved. I went to an altar of prayer in the midst of a glorious revival of religion in my native town. There for three nights I sought the Lord in the pardon of my sins. All who spoke to me told me to believe and nothing was I more anxious to do than to believe; yet no one told me what to believe.[30]

In this paper I will discuss three possible objects of faith. The first is faith in faith. Francis Schaeffer explained,

> Probably the best way to describe this concept of modern theology is to say that it is faith in faith, rather than faith directed to an object which is actually there. Modern man cannot talk about the object of his faith, only about the faith itself. So he can discuss the existence of his faith and its "size" as it exists against all reason, but that is all. Modern man's faith turns inward. In Christianity the value of faith depends upon the object towards which the faith is directed. The true basis for faith is not the

---

[30]Keen, *Faith Papers*, 21.

faith itself, but the work which Christ finished on the cross.[31]

The second possibility is faith in ourselves. Some people struggle to get saved because they do not actually see themselves as lost sinners. They are trusting in their own goodness, what they "had to do" to get saved, how long they sought, or how strict their personal convictions are. Good works, after salvation, are expected but our faith must always be in Jesus Christ. Ephesians 2:10 must always come *after* vv 8-9, but it must not be omitted. We are created in Christ Jesus *for* good works — but not *because* of good works.

The third and only real possibility is faith in Christ alone. "My hope is built on nothing less than Jesus' blood and righteousness."

More specifically, saving faith is faith in the atoning work of Christ. The righteousness of Christ refers to his sinlessness, which was a prerequisite for him to become our substitute. However, our faith must be placed in his atonement of the cross. There he satisfied the just demands of God's law by becoming our substitute. Paul declared, "May I never boast except in the cross of our Lord Jesus Christ" (Gal 6:14).

Wesley wrote, "Nothing in the Christian system is of greater consequence than the doctrine of Atonement."[32] The atonement is universal in its scope, contingent upon the condition of faith being met in the sinner. Every sinner must trust in the work of Christ in order to be saved.

Specifically, that work of Christ was substitutionary.

---

[31]Schaeffer, *The God Who Is There*, 85.

[32]Wesley, *Letter* to Mary Bishop, 7 Feb 1778.

Substitution is prefigured as early as Genesis 22:8. Substitution is clearly foreseen by Isaiah 53:5. According to 2 Corinthians 5:21 Christ became a sin offering for us. The blood of Jesus is a metaphor referring to his life (Deut 12:23). His shed blood graphically portrays him giving his life in substitute for our life.

The purpose of substitution is propitiation. This word *propitiate* can carry a pagan meaning of appeasement. But this meaning is foreign to the New Testament. God satisfies the just demands of his holy law through Christ. "And he himself is the propitiation for our sins, and not for ours only but also for the sins of the whole world" (1 John 2:2).

The purpose of propitiation is satisfaction of the justice of God. We are under the sentence of death because of our sins. Satisfaction of God's law was provided through substitution. According to Romans 3:26 God maintained his justice and upheld his law, while at the same time justified guilty sinners.

The atonement is the ultimate expression of God's love for mankind. Christ also triumphed over the claims of Satan (1 Cor 15:24-25, Col 2:15). To plead the blood means we claim the victory of the cross (John 12:31-33) and the redemption from sin. Thus, our faith is in another and not in ourselves. Our faith is in Christ alone. But we know next to nothing about Christ except through the Holy Scriptures. John said he wrote in order that we might believe that Jesus is the Christ, the Son of God, and that by believing we might have life in his name (John 20:31). Therefore, we must believe in the revelation of God through his written Word, as well as the revelation of God through his Son, the living Word.

Fourth Paper. Justification by Faith

John Wesley agreed with Martin Luther, that the church stands or falls with this doctrine of justification by faith.[33] Wesley himself had been an ordained clergyman for thirteen years before he was born again at Aldersgate. The missing element in Wesley's devotion prior to Aldersgate was the necessity of faith.

Luther's *Preface* to the book of Romans was read at a Moravian society meeting at Aldersgate Street in London on May 24, 1738. John Wesley was present and testified that

> about a quarter before nine, while he was describing the change which God works in the heart through faith in Christ, I felt my heart strangely warmed. I felt I did trust in Christ, Christ alone for salvation, and an assurance was given me that he had taken away my sins, even mine, and saved me from the law of sin and death.[34]

Although Luther's *Preface* defines several key terms and then summarizes each chapter in Romans, the section being read at Wesley's conversion was where "Luther teaches what faith is, and also that faith alone justifies."[35] In that section

---

[33]Wesley, *Journal*, 1 Dec 1767; "The Lord our Righteousness," Sermon #20, ¶ 4.

[34]Wesley, *Journal*, 24 May 1738.

[35]Tyerman, *Life and Times of John Wesley*, 1:180.

Luther wrote:

Faith is not the human notion and dream that some people call faith. When they see that no improvement of life and no good works follow — they fall into the error of saying, "Faith is not enough; one must do works in order to be righteous and be saved." This is due to the fact that when they hear the gospel, they get busy and by their own powers create an idea in their heart which says, "I believe"; they take this then to be a true faith. But, as it is a human figment and idea that never reaches the depths of the heart, nothing comes of it either, and no improvement follows.

Faith, however, is a divine work in us which changes us and makes us to be born anew of God, John 1:12-13. It kills the old Adam and makes us altogether different men, in heart and spirit and mind and powers; and it brings with it the Holy Spirit. It is a living, busy, active, mighty thing, this faith. It is impossible for it not to be doing good works incessantly. It does not ask whether good works are to be done, but before the question is asked, it has already done them, and is constantly doing them. Whoever does not do such works, however, is an unbeliever. He gropes and looks around for faith and good works, but knows neither what faith is nor what good works are. Yet he talks and talks, with many works, about faith and good works.

Faith is a living, daring confidence in God's grace, so sure and certain that the believer would stake his life on it a thousand times. This knowledge of and confidence in God's grace makes men glad and bold and happy in dealing with God and with all creatures. And this is the work which the Holy Spirit performs in faith. Because of it, without compulsion, a person is ready and glad to do good to everyone, to serve everyone, to suffer everything, out of love and praise to God who has shown him this grace. Thus it is impossible to separate works from faith, quite as impossible as to separate heat and light from fire.

Beware, therefore, of your own false notions and of idle talkers who imagine themselves wise enough to make decisions about faith and good works, and yet are the greatest fools. Pray God that he may work faith in you. Otherwise, you will surely remain forever without faith, regardless of what you may think or do.[36]

Calvinism, however, refers to this concept of active faith as *voluntarism*. Calvin did not accept a voluntaristic faith. His followers taught that faith was passively received. Thus, the debate is whether faith is an act of the will or it is a passive persuasion of the mind. The term used to describe faith as an act of the will is "voluntarism." It seems to me a better term would be "volitionalism," meaning faith was an act of man's will, his volition, or choice.

There is a sense in which faith is a gift, yet we must avoid conflating faith and assurance. Calvin taught that we know we are elect if we have an inner persuasion, based on the premise that faith is only given to the elect. However, this view that faith is passive leaves unanswered questions, especially when coupled with an emphasis on a temporary faith. How do those with an inner persuasion know whether this is

---

[36]Luther, *Works*, 35:370-371.

a temporary faith, whether it is "common grace," an external and "ineffectual calling"?

Jacob Arminius explained that the believer can really "fall from that very grace wherewith God embraces him unto life eternal."[37] According to Arminius, if the believer does not persevere, such a person proves to be non-elect. The difference is that Calvin taught that believers persevere because they are elected. Arminius, on the other hand, taught that God elects believers whom he foresees will persevere.

However, faith cannot be totally monergistic, whether it comes before or after regeneration. *Monergism* means that only one person is working. While it is true that God initiates the process, through preliminary grace he enables us to respond. Thus, the process is *synergistic*. Otherwise, justification is actually by divine decree and not by faith. Wesley argued that if salvation is by absolute decree, it is not by works, but neither is it by faith. "For *unconditional* decree excludes faith as well as works."[38]

In 2010 I presented a paper at the Wesleyan Studies track of the Evangelical Theological Society meeting. The "debate" format included a response from Michael Horton. To my surprise Horton seemed to pull away from the idea that we are justified by faith. He said that we are not actually justified by faith, but by Christ. But this is not the language of Romans 5:1. He explained that he interprets "justification by faith" as shorthand for saying that salvation is by Christ and his works rather than our merits.

While I agree that we are saved by the finished work of Christ and not through our own merits, I suspect that we mean

---

[37]Arminius, *Works*, 3:460.

[38]Wesley, *BE Works*, 13:554.

something different by *faith*. Is faith active or passive? Horton cautions that faith can become a meritorious work, but I fail to see how actively and completely trusting in the work of another is meritorious. Faith cannot be meritorious since faith consists in renouncing all merit and trusting in another. Horton says that the Westminster Confession of Faith cautions against this. Yet I do not accept the Westminster Confession as the litmus test of orthodoxy

The Westminster Confession declares that God imputes the obedience and satisfaction of Christ. Thus, faith is passive. Horton seems to assert that the elect are real subjects in the acts of faith and repentance. But in the Calvinistic order of salvation, faith and repentance come *after* regeneration. My concern remains, "Faith cannot be reduced to the righteousness of Christ which the elect passively have imputed to their account as evidence of their regeneration."[39]

It seems that in this view the elect were saved when in the counsel of God, he decreed their election. *Faith*, then is the revelation of that selection. Therefore the "witness of the Spirit" to Calvinists is a witness of election, not salvation. Calvin taught that the elect have assurance they were chosen because they were given faith. Calvin taught that faith was a passive assurance, assurance to what God had already done in Christ. Since only the elect were given faith, faith itself is assurance. This amounts to a persuasion of being in the elect, however, and not the realization at that moment of present salvation. To him faith was an involuntary, passive persuasion of the mind. In the Calvinistic order of salvation we are first regenerated, then we believe. Thus, faith and assurance are one and the same. Faith, then, is the consequence of election,

---

[39]Stated in my unpublished paper, "Justification: Imputed *and* Imparted: A Survey of Romans," 9.

not the condition for salvation. Faith informs, it does not obtain. This surfaces as the major difference between Calvinism and Arminianism on faith. Yet Scripture seems clear, "Believe in the Lord Jesus Christ and you will be saved" (Acts 16:31).

Forlines argued that a passive faith, which bypasses the personality, cannot be true faith at all. "There can be no faith on the part of a human being without the active involvement of his personality. It is a contradiction of the facts of human personality to think that a person can believe and it be totally the work of God with no human involvement."[40]

Wesleyanism, as usual, is a mediating position between the extremes of a presumptuous faith which leads to antinomianism and a passive faith which leads to fatalism. In contrast to Calvinism, we emphasize that faith is the condition of salvation and that we must believe in order to be justified. Prevenient or preliminary grace enables us to respond. In that sense, no one can believe without enabling grace. And this preliminary grace provides the gift of faith. But faith is not entirely passive. Faith is the condition for salvation and God will not believe for us. We are enabled by prevenient grace to believe when we have repented and the direct witness of the Spirit is the response to true saving faith. But we must believe. Between the initial assurance that Christ loved me and the concluding conviction that I am saved, I must actively, and with complete abandonment, trust in him. Wesley concluded, "Now, at this instant, in the present moment, and in thy present state, sinner as thou art, just as thou art, believe the gospel."[41]

---

[40]Forlines, "Election in Romans 9," 7-8.

[41]Wesley, "The Righteousness of Faith," 3.6.

Assurance is the divine response to true faith and that assurance is further corroborated by the indirect assurance of a holy life. Joseph Sutcliffe stated that the reflex or indirect assurance does follow, but he refused to reduce assurance to nothing more than an indirect assurance.

The witness of the Spirit is no reflex act whatever; it is God himself shining on the soul, as a reconciled Father, dispersing doubts and fears from the mind. The reflex acts follow, and associate with the witness of our own spirit, that we have wept for sin, implored mercy, and believed on the Savior, whose love is now shed abroad in the heart.[42]

---

[42]Sutcliffe, *Commentary*, 2:576.

Fifth Paper. Abraham -
The Father of Faith

Hebrews 11 is considered the "faith chapter" and Abraham is the leading example. But Romans 4 is also a "faith chapter" and in some ways goes deeper in demonstrating how faith works. Abraham's faith looked forward to the day when Christ would come (John 8:56). Our faith looks back at his finished work. Yet the function of faith was the same. "These words were written not for him alone but also for us" (Rom 4:23-24). The life of Abraham exemplifies how we live by faith.

Four thousand years ago God called Abram out of Ur of Chaldea. Abram lived in a pagan and idolatrous city of about 300,000. These people were highly educated and had a system of writing. Ur was an important commercial city located on the Euphrates River about a hundred miles northwest of the Persian Gulf. In 1922 a British archeologist, Leonard Wooley, discovered they had two-story homes with indoor plumbing and tile drains down through the streets.

They worshiped a multitude of gods, but foremost was the moon. We know from Joshua 24:2 that Abram's father was such an idolater. But the promise of God came to Abram. "I have made you a father of many nations"(Gen 17:5). His name was changed at that time to Abraham, which means "father of many." However, the promise first came to Abram in Genesis 12, twenty-four years earlier. Paul quoted from Genesis 17 to demonstrate that Abraham *had already been made* a father of many nations *before* his circumcision (Gen 17:10). Thus, Abram was justified by faith and not by circumcision.

At 75 Abram left all that was familiar to him. He would lead his flocks around the desert some 1200 miles to Palestine. For the rest of his life he would live in a tent.

We can learn from Abraham's life of faith. The process of faith begins with grace. At that time Abram was a pagan in Ur. God did two things (Rom 4:17):

- God gave life to the dead. God is the one who quickens or makes alive. God revealed himself and gave faith to Abram. According to Romans 10:17 "faith comes through the Word." God gives us faith by speaking either directly or through his Word. Where people have access to the Scriptures, he usually speaks through them. Notice that the promise of God was spoken to Abram but written to us. It really makes no difference. The written Word is just as authoritative as the spoken word.

- God calls things that are not as though they were. God is actually calling this pagan man the father of a great nation. This is not predestination; it is foreknowledge. God is saying, *if* you will obey me by leaving Ur and *if* you will enter into a covenant with me, I will make you a father of many.

But Abram is not yet justified. God has revealed himself and called Abram, but that call is not irresistible. God reveals himself, to some degree, to everyone. John 1:9 teaches that God gives at least some light to everyone. Jesus taught that "many are called, but few are chosen" (Matt 22:14). Most people do not respond, but Abram did. He believed (Rom 4:17). When Abram believed, his faith was credited to him as righteousness (v 9). God made him righteous, not by his works, but by faith alone. We are not saved *because* of our faith. We are saved by grace (v 16). God accepts our faith *for* righteousness, but we are saved *because* of his grace.

Faith comes from God, but we must believe. The proof that Abram believed is that he obeyed — he left Ur. And when Paul takes up the account twenty-four years later, Abraham is *still* believing. At this point he is circumcised as a sign and seal of the covenant God makes with him.

Verses 3, 17-18 all state that Abraham believed. Against all natural circumstances, he chose to believe. What were those circumstances? In v 19 he faced the fact that his body was as good as dead. He was a hundred years old. He also faced the fact that Sarah's womb was also dead at ninety.

Faith in not a leap into the dark. It is not irrational. It is not saying something is true even when the facts speak otherwise. I am not saved or healed because I declare that I am. Rather, I face the facts that my circumstances are impossible. I cannot save or heal myself. Physical circumstances militate against faith in the promise of God. But God has spoken and he has given me faith. I look at my circumstances on the one hand, but I look at his promise on the other hand and I choose to stand on his promise. There can be no faith where there is no promise. "No faith in God is really valid unless it involves faith in a specific revelation or promise of God."[43] But we can stand on his Word and act upon what he reveals.

Abraham did not waver through unbelief regarding the promise of God (v 20). To waver or stagger really means to be divided in our minds, to hesitate or to doubt. Satan will raise questions — "did God really say that?"

How do we keep on believing? In v 20 Abraham "was strengthened in his faith and gave glory to God." Abraham was not strengthened by *his* faith; rather, his faith was

---

[43]Schaeffer, *The Finished Work of Christ*, 89.

strengthened by God. "Strengthen me according to your word" (Ps 119:28).

How does God strengthen our faith? God empowers us as we give glory to him. This is the power of praise. Abraham has already believed God and God has justified him, but he must keep on believing. So must we.

According to v 5 we maintain our justification by trusting God. Here *believing* is in the present tense. Verse 11 also teaches that righteousness is imputed to us *as we believe.* Verse 24 teaches that for those who keep on believing, righteousness will be credited to them.

The Greek word λογίζομαι (*logizomai*) occurs eleven times in this chapter. It means to reckon, credit, rank with, calculate, consider, deliberate, grasp, draw a logical conclusion, decide, or impute. It is a bookkeeping metaphor, but a legal act. Our faith in the substitutionary atonement of Christ is imputed to us for righteousness.

> When God imputes faith for righteousness, he has respect, not to the worthiness or excellency of Faith, but to the worthiness and excellency of that Divine Redeemer on whom our faith terminates.[44]

But God does not merely impute righteousness; he also imparts the Holy Spirit who enables us to keep the commandments.

So how does the believer glorify God? We focus on his nature and his attributes. He gives life to the dead (v 17). Twenty-four years into this faith journey, Abraham and Sarah are more dead than alive. His name means the father of *many*, but thus far he is not yet the father of *any*. How does he

---

[44]Bunting, *Justification by Faith*, 30.

reconcile all this? Abraham does not focus on the problem, but on the power of God.

Time passes and Isaac, the promise, grows to manhood. Again God speaks. "Take Isaac, your only son, whom you love and sacrifice him." This is the first time the word *love* occurs in the Bible. He loved Isaac, but he trusted God. How did Abraham keep faith in the greatest crisis of his life? He glorified God who gives life to the dead. According to Hebrews 11:19 he did receive Isaac back from the dead, figuratively speaking.

We have even more reason to glorify God because he raised Jesus our Lord from the dead (v 24). For those who do believe and are assailed by doubts and fear, the God who has power over death can do anything.

And so we grow in faith by giving glory to God who has power over death *and* who calls things that are not as though they were. He calls into being what does not exist as easily as he calls that which does exist. In the beginning God spoke into nothing (*ex nihilo*) and said, "Let there be." Everything which now exists came into being.

Can we call something which is not as thought it is? Some teach that is faith, but it is really presumption. Yet God can do it because he is God. In his foreknowledge he knows what he has planned to do and he has the power to make it happen. But it won't work for us to "name-it-and-claim it" for the simply fact that we are *not* God.

Worship expresses faith. We glorify him by praising him for his acts of creation and resurrection. We continue to believe him and he continues to strengthen our faith.

When we were dead in our trespasses and sins, he declares that if we will believe him he will justify us. Then he begins to recreate us, making us what we were not. A God who can transform dead sinners like we once were can do anything!

Abraham learned to look away from the problem and look up to the promise. According to v 20 his faith never wavered. But in Genesis 17:17 he asked after twenty-four years, "Will a son be born to a man a hundred years old? Will Sarah bear a child at the age of ninety?" Is his faith wavering? No, he is just stating the facts. Romans 4:20 states that he did not waver *through unbelief*. He did not understand, but he kept believing. As the testing became more severe, his faith also grew stronger.

How do we know that he did not lose faith? He asked that Ishmael would *also* be protected and blessed (Gen 17:18). This implies that he is aware that God has not yet fulfilled his promise. He laughs in wonder at how God will keep his promise. However, Sarah doubted, laughed, and then lied (Gen 18:12-15). Abraham laughs as he anticipates the future. But Sarah is in denial. As Abraham kept on believing God strengthened his faith until he was fully persuaded (v 21). This word πληροφορέω (*plerophoreo*) means fully convinced or wholly certain. Wesley taught this full assurance of faith is "the common privilege of Christians."[45]

Richard Watson wrote that such an assurance was attainable and every Christian ought to seek it. "This, however, does not exclude occasional doubt and weakness of faith, from the earlier stages of his experience."[46] In other words there are stages of faith. Abraham did not receive the full assurance of faith until twenty-four years after he first believed (Gen 17:19-21). We must not waver; we must worship. God will strengthen our faith until we reach a level where we

---

[45]Wesley, *Letter* to Dr. Rutherforth, 28 March 1768.

[46]Watson, *Dictionary*, 101.

are fully persuaded by his promises. Charles Wesley wrote,

> Through unbelief I stagger not,
> For God hath spoken the word.
> Faith, mighty faith, the promise sees,
> And looks to that alone;
> laughs at impossibilities
> And cries, It shall be done.[47]

---

[47]Wesley, *BE Works*, 7:516, hymn #350.

Throughout Scripture, the promises of prosperity are always made to the covenant keepers (see Deut 28, Ps 1:3; Prov 28:13). If we fully obey the Lord, we will become the head and not the tail (Deut 28:13). In his explanation of Deuteronomy 28, Victor Hamilton wrote that

> those who follow the Lord may anticipate blessing in the form of children, health, prosperity, conquest over the enemy, or ideal climatic conditions in which to produce agricultural crops. Conversely, the absence of these benefits, or the presence of their antithesis, is a result of disobedience to covenantal norms.[48]

These promises are not made to those who name-it-and-claim-it. Rather, they are made to those who are in covenant with God.

Thus, the so-called faith teachers have an inadequate grasp of the Word. They are teaching a type of magic and calling it "faith." This is inadequate because it fails to link the means with the end. True prosperity is realized only by those who keep covenant with God.

It also amounts to reductionism because biblical prosperity is the peace or shalom of God, wisdom and understanding from God, positive relationships, a loving family, and hope for the future. They have reduced all of this to material prosperity.

---

[48]Hamilton, *Handbook on the Pentateuch*, 446.

Charles Farah concluded that much of what passes for faith today is in fact presumption. "Failure to distinguish the difference between these two has caused untold anguish to thousands of sincere and dedicated Spirit-filled Christians for whom the ordinary formulas have not worked."[49] The modern teaching of faith as a leap in the dark is based on presumption. This is faith in faith.[50]

Prosperity teachers claim that words create reality. Words are the containers of faith. They are magical. Even God cannot do anything except by faith. They teach that the substance God used in Hebrews 11:1 was faith. But God created and sustains everything through the word of his power (Heb 1:3). Yet Kenneth Copeland declared, "Faith is a power force. It is a tangible force. It is a conductive force."[51] He teaches that faith is God's source of power.[52]

Yet Jesus taught that we were to have faith *in God* (Mark 11:22). The object of our faith matters! Kenneth Copeland taught, "God is a faith being" and that man operates in the same way God operates.[53] But does this mean faith in God or in faith? And in whom would God put his faith?

John Wesley had to deal with Thomas Maxfield, one of his lay preachers, who had taught "Crede quod habes et habes" — "believe that you have [perfection] and you have." While Maxfield considered this formula the equivalent of

---

[49]Farah, *From the Pinnacle of the Temple*, 205.

[50]For example, Charles Capps, *How to Have Faith in Your Faith* (1986).

[51]Copeland, *The Force of Faith*, 10.

[52]Copeland, *Freedom from Fear*, 12.

[53]McConnell, *A Different Gospel*,141.

Mark 11:24, John Fletcher wrote that "the humble reason of the believer, and the irrational presumption of the enthusiast, draws this doctrine to the right hand or to the left. But to split the hair—here lies the difficulty."[54]

John Wesley taught that the Holy Spirit brought assurance of entire sanctification and that this assurance was verified indirectly by the fruit of the Spirit and a holy life. Thus, Methodism held that true faith produces evidence.

In contrast, Phoebe Palmer was a primary influence within the American holiness movement. She taught there was a shorter way to sanctification. The seeker was instructed: (1) put your all on the altar; (2) Christ is the altar; (3) the altar, Christ, sanctifies the gift. Therefore, if the seeker has put all on the altar, he or she is sanctified. The result was a substitution of presumption for faith and the adoption of a theological syllogism: I am sanctified because I say I am. There is no divine assurance, but the certainty is based on a kind of auto-suggestion.

Palmer's instruction is based upon the logical deduction that, if the seeker has put all on the altar, he or she is sanctified. The seeker has a duty to believe this even if there is not further evidence of sanctification. She taught that if the seeker will, he may exercise faith. If he may exercise faith, then he may exercise faith when he wills. Therefore, faith is an obligation at the very moment of consecration. To hesitate is to question the integrity of God. Such doubting constitutes sin and causes the seeker to lose the blessing of justification. Thus, Palmer described faith as "omnipotent." In fact she taught, "The act, on your part, must necessarily induce the

---

[54]Fletcher, *Works*, 4:317.

promised result on the part of God."[55] According to historian David Bebbington, "A new era had dawned in holiness teaching."[56]

Palmer's "name-it-and-claim-it" theology was opposed by many in her day, especially by Bishop Nathan Bangs, who said it was "unsound, unscriptural, anti-Wesleyan and no doubt in many cases had caused deception."[57] Yet it is the opinion of Timothy Smith that by 1867, "her views had won out."[58]

Thomas Oden concluded that Palmer was the link between Methodism and Pentecostalism.[59] The emphasis that Palmer placed upon claiming and verbally affirming sanctification as a means of receiving it was transferred by E. W. Kenyon to health and wealth.[60]

The faith teachers claim that through the "creative word" you can create your own reality through the power of positive confession. What Copeland calls "positive confession" is the same technique that the occult world calls "creative visualization." The power of thinking was believed to even be able to create or destroy physical reality. This revelation knowledge is superior to sense or empirical knowledge. Copeland describes faith as a force which is released by our words. Charles Capps said, "Words are the most powerful thing in

---

[55]Palmer, *Faith and Its Effects*, 29, 98, 101-104, 132.

[56]Bebbington, *The Dominance of Evangelicalism*, 203.

[57]Stevens, *Life and Times of Nathan Bangs,* 396-402.

[58]Smith, *Revivalism and Social Reform*, 125.

[59]Oden, "Phoebe Palmer as the Missing Link," 16-19.

[60]Simmons, *E. W. Kenyon*, 158-159, 171-172.

the universe."[61]

Sometimes Job 22:28 is cited as a biblical basis for de-creeing wealth, but God said that Eliphaz had *not* spoken what was right (Job 42:7). The Bible contains over four hundred verses on the use and abuse of money. Thus we do not decree wealth, but wealth is gained by following the principles of stewardship.

Danny McCain observed, "For every positive reference to wealth in the New Testament there are 10 negative statements about wealth. The New Testament writers recognized the danger of wealth. It has a way of drawing a person away from God."[62]

Yet Charles Capps taught that we set in motion spiritual laws by what we say and that if applied correctly, everything we say will come to pass.[63] Thus, we are taught that we can command God and that he is obligated to heal because of our confession of faith. A. A. Allen once boasted that he could command God to turn dollar bills into twenty dollar bills.[64] Kenneth Copeland wrote, "As a believer, you have a right to make commands in the name of Jesus. Each time you stand on the Word, you are commanding God to a certain extent."[65] However, there is a division of labor between the Creator and his creation. God gives the commands and we obey *his* commands.

All this emphasis on the creative word is based on a

---

[61]Capps, *The Tongue*, 7.

[62]McCain, "Prosperity: A Biblical Perspective," 64.

[63]Capps, *The Tongue*, 22,131-132.

[64]Liardon, *God's Generals*, 408-410.

[65]Copeland, *Our Covenant with God*, 32.

misunderstanding of *rhema* (ῥῆμα). The word *rhema* is used five times in Romans 10, but this chapter does not support the faith doctrine of the prosperity teachers. We are to confess with the tongue what has happened in the heart by the Holy Spirit. The confession without the reality will not create the reality.

It is asserted that God has set up certain laws in his universe. Among these are the laws on wealth and health. Believers activate these laws by speaking them with their own mouths. Everything we decree will come to pass. Kaiser listed the most popular Old Testament texts: Exodus 15:26; Joshua 1:8; Job 36:11; Psalm 34:10, 35:27, 37:25, 103:3; Isaiah 53:4-5. These material promises were made to Israel corporately to teach the nations that it was God producing Israel's wealth. These blessings were to be shared and used as teaching tools.

"However, these texts do not constitute an adequate basis for placing some type of magical power in the words themselves." Just because דבר (*debar*) can be translated as either *word* or *thing*, does not mean that once a word is uttered it can become a thing.

Kaiser concluded that the message of health, wealth, and prosperity fails on the very texts and theological principles it wishes to establish. "There is not basis for a so-called power of the word apart from the only One who can fill that word with power, our Lord Jesus himself."[66]

Yet C. S. Lovett wrote that God's healing power is available through our own mind and we can trigger it by faith. "If you had direct access to your unconscious mind, you could

---

[66]Kaiser, "Old Testament Promise of Material Blessings and the Contemporary Believer," 151-170.

command any disease to be healed in a flash."[67] This statement illustrates the difference between faith healing and divine healing. Do we heal ourselves by speaking healing into reality, or are we healed by a touch from Jehovah Rapha?

Certainly God cares about our well-being, as indicated in 3 John 2. However, this Greek word εὐοδόω (euodoo) simply meant to go well, and does not refer to financial wealth.[68] Physical healing is a foretaste of the resurrection of the body. If God has the power to raise from the dead, he has power to heal the sick. For the child of God, the future breaks into the present, in the kingdom of God. We know the kingdom has come because we have tasted the power of the world to come (Heb 6:5). And while divine healing is now possible, then there will be a general resurrection.

In the mean time, the influence of the gospel will bring healing to the nations of the world. Thus, the healing through Christ extends beyond mere physical healing which would be temporary and personal. Second Chronicles 7:14 promises the healing of the land of God's covenant people. God will flood this world with his Spirit and bring healing to the nations (Rev 22:2; Ezek 47:1-12).

Yet the Manifest Sons of God movement taught, as did Kenyon, that through this gnostic faith God is creating a super-race of elite overcomers.[69] This teaching that we are gods can also be found in the Manifest Sons of God and the writings of E. W. Kenyon, William Branham, and John G. Lake.

The Manifest Sons of God movement also taught free-

---

[67]Lovett, "The Medicine of Your Mind."

[68]Sarles, "Theological Evaluation of the Prosperity Gospel," 338.

[69]McConnell, A Different Gospel, 21.

dom from death. Here they clearly confused the *already* with the *not yet*. We are *already* in the kingdom and have tasted the power of the world to come (Heb 6:5); but we are still under the curse of sin, and our bodies will die regardless of what we confess.

The doctrine of *rhema* is name-it-and-claim-it. You can have what you confess."What I confess, I possess."[70] This is the positive confession teaching. But we cannot create a new reality by speaking it into existence.

Dan McConnell demonstrated that Kenneth Hagin plagiarized the bulk of his theology from E. W. Kenyon (1867-1948).[71] However, Hagin claimed that "the Holy Spirit gave him the same words as Kenyon with his having prior knowledge of the sources!"[72]

McConnell also asserted that the roots of Kenyon's theology can be traced to metaphysical cults, such as New Thought and Christian Science. "New Thought" was the creation of Phineas P. Quimby (1802-1866) and was a banner under which a variety of teachings united.

The common element was a belief that the spiritual realm is the only true reality and the cause of every physical effect. Thus, we must use our mind to create and control our own reality. Mary Baker Eddy, the founder of Christian Science, was influenced greatly by Quimby.

Judith Matta was the first person to make this assertion in 1984. She was assisted by the faculty at Biola University's Talbot School of Theology to produce *The Born Again Jesus*

---

[70]Kenyon, *The Hidden Man*, 98; Hagin, *Bible Faith Study Course*, 92; Capps, *Releasing the Ability of God*, 67.

[71]McConnell, *A Different Gospel*, 3-14.

[72]Synan, "Faith of Kenneth Hagin," 68.

of the Word-Faith Teaching. McConnell built upon her research and Hank Hanegraff popularized it in *Christianity in Crisis.*

However, in 1997 Joe McIntyre first published a rebuttal, *E. W. Kenyon and His Message of Faith: The True Story.* McIntyre argues that Kenyon did not form his teaching from cultic sources. McIntyre argues that Kenyon's views were formed by mainstream holiness and Keswick teachers such as Phoebe Palmer, Charles Cullis, Alexander Dowie, A. B. Simpson, Andrew Murray, D. L. Moody, and Kelso Carter.[73]

Since the purpose of this excursus is to expose doctrinal error, it is not necessary to trace historically all of the blame for current excesses in the faith movement to Kenyon or to determine the source of Kenyon's thought. However, McIntyre does emphasize the fact that Kenyon was profoundly influenced by the teachings of Phoebe Palmer and argues that Palmer was teaching her views on faith prior to the rise of metaphysical cults. In my book *Holy Living* I devote 18 pages to show how Palmer departed from the teachings of John Wesley.[74]

There may be plenty of blame to go around. Dennis Hollinger wrote that McConnell's book, *A Different Gospel,* attempts to undermine the Pentecostal influence of the prosperity gospel, giving primacy to the "Kenyon Connection." Hollinger, however, felt that the role of the healing revivalist tradition cannot be minimized.[75] But elsewhere Hollinger observed, "Various Pentecostal healing evangelists of the 1940s and the 1950s had read Kenyon's works and at times

---

[73]McIntyre, *E. W. Kenyon and His Message of Faith* (2010).

[74]Reasoner, *Holy Living,* 2:544-562.

[75]Hollinger, "Enjoying God Forever," 1:40.

quoted from him."[76]

The modern faith healers hold a form of gnosticism which teaches that all reality and all causality is determined in the spiritual realm. This is *metaphysical*, meaning above the physical. The only true reality is spiritual reality, and this is the cause of every effect in the physical.

There is a lack of connection between the "faith" teachers and historic Christianity. Their teaching can be traced back to ancient gnosticism and its emphasis on knowledge as the basis for salvation. Rather than trust in God, faith is a metaphysical force by which we create our health and wealth. And we may fall into sickness or financial trouble by our lack of faith.

The prosperity teaching on seed faith is that we can materialize our thoughts of success, prosperity, and abundance by sowing our best financial seed. Oral Roberts taught, "The seed of giving is the seed of faith! And the seed has to be planted before we can speak to our mountain of need to be removed."[77]

Passages such as 2 Corinthians 9:6-15 and Galatians 6:7-9 are often cited. Then we are told that we have the potential within us and if we will release it, God will make it grow. Thus we are encouraged to put our faith to work, to take the leap of faith, and expect God to work. Faith is said to be activated by giving beyond our means to a faith teacher.

But our giving should be motivated by thanksgiving for what God has given us, not in anticipation of what God will give us. I do not give in order to receive. We do not force God to act in obligation to us. Giving is an act of obedience and an

---

[76]Hollinger, "Enjoying God Forever," 2:23.

[77]Roberts, *Daily Guide to Miracles*, 63.

expression of worship.

Scripture compares faith to a seed, but never teaches seed faith giving in order to expect a miracle. Oral Roberts claimed this was revealed to him from Acts 20:35, but the verse does not teach what he claimed. He taught the greater the seed sown, the more God has to work with. But we do not write our own ticket with God, although that is the teaching of Kenneth Hagin.[78] Instead, we obey what God has written!

Today the new apostolic false prophets teach that if we want wealth we have to give to them first because God's blessing flows down from heaven through them.[79] We are to pay up front and except a miracle. In God's economy, however, the tithe is the firstfruits of what we *have* received (Prov 3:9-10) not a spiritual bet which we hope to win.

Roberts taught that God responds primarily to our faith, especially when it is verbalized. This emphasis on the power of words was borrowed from E. W. Kenyon.[80] It also implies a distinction between *rhema,* the spoken word, and *logos*, the recorded word of Scripture. This *rhema* doctrine is taught as

---

[78]The actual title of a book by Kenneth Hagin is *How to Write Your Own Ticket with God* (1979).

[79]Hinn, *God, Greed, and the (Prosperity) Gospel*, 47; Pivec and Geivett, *Counterfeit Kingdom*, 80-86; Hanegraaf, *Christianity in Crisis*, 211.

[80]Gossett and Kenyon, *The Power of Your Words* (1977). See McConnell, *A Different Gospel*. McConnell is accused of misrepresenting Kenyon by McIntyre, *E. W. Kenyon and His Message of Faith*, 318-325. Part of McIntyre's rebuttal consists in showing that American holiness teachers, such as Phoebe Palmer, taught essentially what Kenyon taught. However, I would also reject Phoebe Palmer's teaching on faith.

creative. "What I confess, I possess."[81]

Roberts also taught that we already have faith, but we must turn our faith loose."[82] But true faith is primarily our response to God's Word. We do not force his hand. Faith is our response to God's Word. Faith is not a force by which we create health and wealth by speaking them into existence.

---

[81]Kenyon, *The Hidden Man*, 98; Hagin, *Bible Faith Study Course*, 92; Capps, *Releasing the Ability of God*, 67.

[82]Roberts, *God Is a Good God*, 42-47. See also *If You Need Healing Do These Things*, 42 which teaches how to use a point of contact for the release of faith.

Seventh Paper. Living by Faith

Faith is not a one-time act. The commands to have faith are usually in the present tense.[83] We are justified by faith, and the justified live by that same faith (Hab 2:4). We must have faith in order to please God (Heb 11:6). We must continue in the faith (Col 1:23). According to Romans 12:3 every Christian has been given a measure of faith. The context is clearly referring to believers. The same God has given each of us different gifts. Therefore we have nothing to boast of, since these gifts — even faith itself — comes from God.

Not to be confused, according to 1 Corinthians 12:9-11 the gift of faith is one of the gifts of the Spirit. While all faith has its source in God, this particular gift is faith for a particular situation. Examples are cited in Hebrews 11:33-35. George Müller (1805-1898) exemplified this gift of faith.[84] This gift could also be associated with God-given vision for ministry.

There are levels of faith. A survey of the Scriptures reveal that some have little faith (Matt 6:30), while others have great faith (Matt 8:10). Therefore, we should all pray that God will increase our faith (Luke 17:5). Our faith is increased when we are put in situations where we must trust God and

---

[83]See Appendix B.

[84]Müller, *The Life of Trust* (1860); *The Autobiography of George Müller* (1905).

we choose to do so.

Living by faith is obedience to the commands of Christ. How does this differ from legalism? Properly defined, legalism substitutes works for faith. "In legalism keeping the law becomes an end in itself rather than a means to the service of God and fellow humanity."[85]

On the other hand, antinomianism, or lawlessness, substitutes faith for works. We can never save ourselves through our good works, yet we should never presume that we are saved while living in disobedience to the Word. Martin Luther discovered that his monastic works were filthy rags in the sight of God. However, he did not find the proper balance between faith and works. Luther taught that man was at the same time just and yet sinful (*simul justus et peccator*).

Wesley concluded, "Who has wrote more ably than Martin Luther on justification by faith alone? And who was more ignorant of the doctrine of sanctification, or more confused in his conceptions of it?"[86] Donald Bloesch explained, "We must not make the mistake of thinking that we can live without the law. Christ did not come to abolish the law, but to fulfill it (Matt 5:17)."[87]

Living by faith is choosing to trust God in all circumstances. I choose to stand on God's Word and trust in his providence. God will keep in perfect peace whomever has his mind stayed on God. This steadfast mind is referenced in Isaiah 26:3. The Hebrew verb is סמך (*samak*), meaning to prop, lean on, or take hold of. This is a spiritual discipline.

---

[85] Bleosch, *Faith and Its Counterfeits*, 25.

[86] Wesley, "On God's Vineyard," Sermon #107, 1.5; see also Wesley, *Journal*, 15 June 1741.

[87] Bloesch, *Faith and Its Counterfeits*, 32.

Our mind is at peace when we are leaning completely on God. "Great peace have they who love your law, and nothing can make them stumble" (Ps 119:165). The KJV says nothing shall *offend* or cause to stumble. This is a metaphor. We are not talking about falling in the literal sense. Thus, we could say that nothing shall *upset* them. But we do stumble and lose our peace when our thoughts are not centered upon God's Word.

Living by faith means that we take captive every thought inconsistent with faith. Satan is defeated when we learn to think biblically. Proverbs 4:23 teaches us above everything else to *guard* — keep a sharp lookout or protect our heart. The Hebrew word *heart* has no equivalent in English. It can refer to the body's function, the psyche's function, or the spiritual functions. Here it refers to the intellect, emotions, and will. In other words Solomon is teaching us to control our thinking. Everything we do flows from it. Thus, it is the spring or source of life.

This concept corresponds to Proverbs 23:7, "As he thinks within himself, so he is." Solomon was describing a guest eating at the table of a stingy man. The host encourages his guest to eat and drink, but his inward attitude forms his true identity. Thus there is a disconnect between what he says and how he actually feels. Waltke quoted a scholar who explained that his "inscape" determines his landscape.[88]

But the principle of inward reality also has positive application. If I will guard what I dwell upon — what I "download" — determines what malware pops up. I am promised that the peace of God which transcends all understanding will guard my heart and mind in Christ Jesus (Phil 4:6-7) if I guard my mind.

---

[88]Waltke, *Proverbs 15-31*, 242.

God did not give us a spirit of fearfulness (2 Tim 1:7). This word *deilia* describes cowardice and timidity and is never used in a good sense. A synonym, the word *phobia* is used in Romans 8:15. We did not receive the spirit of slavery or bondage which results from such fear. One of the marks of the indwelling Spirit is release from this bondage of fear. But if we accept it, the devil will give it.

According to 2 Timothy 1:7, God gives us or equips us with what we need, which is

- a spirit of power or boldness. We are to be confident in our relationship with God.

- a spirit of love. Love conquers fear. In 1 John 4:18 this is a present tense verb denoting ongoing action.

- a spirit of self discipline or a sound mind. The Greek word is σωφρονισμός (*sophronismos*) which means to save the mind. It describes sound judgment. A cognate word is used in Romans 12:3 and 1 Timothy 3:2. So should it be translated *discipline* or *sound mind*? The root meaning of *sozo* (to save) plus *phren* (the mind) does refer to the rational, reason, or mind. As an adjective, it is related to the noun σωφροσύνη in 1 Timothy 2:9 and 15 which does mean of a sound mind, sane, or in one's senses. The translation *sober* tends to convey a restricted meaning that the subject is not drunk. Yet this right mind conveys much more than a solemn demeanor.

Therefore self-discipline, as enabled by the Spirit, results in me being in my right mind. In our culture everyone has some labeled syndrome, but few exert much self discipline. Our hope — even our salvation — depends upon such self control. The result is that we have sound judgment or that our mind is saved. Thus, the promise is that the Holy Spirit will empower us to be sane, sensible, and self-controlled. This is the fruit of the Spirit (Gal 5:23). The promise of 2 Timothy 1:7 does not imply that we will become intellectual giants, but it does promise that the Holy Spirit will help us use effectively what intellectual resources we do possess.

Thus, part of Christian maturity is attaining an emotional and mental balance. It is included in the shalom which God has promised us. A gospel song says, "I'm living by faith and feel no alarm." Such maturity comes by living and growing in faith. This life of faith encompasses our whole personality. Intellectuality, I cannot entertain any thought which doubts God's word. Volitionally, I keep covenant with God by keeping his law. Emotionally, as I lean on and trust in the Lord, he gives me his peace which results in the salvation of my mind.

Eighth Paper.
Entire Sanctification by Faith

Romans 1:17 tells us that God has revealed in the gospel a righteousness that is "by faith from first to last." Literally it reads "from faith to faith." Preaching "on the discoveries of faith," Wesley exhorted the hearer to "press on by all possible means, till he passes 'from faith to faith'; from the faith of a servant to the faith of a son; from the spirit of bondage unto fear, to the spirit of childlike love."

Just as God revealed himself to the world a little at a time, so he reveals himself in our lives in the same way. John divides the family of God into three groups: young children, young men, and fathers (1 John 2:12-14).

It is possible to receive even more grace than we experience in the new birth. This perfecting grace was provided for in the atonement. The blood of Jesus Christ can cleanse from all sin (1 John 1:7). According to v 9 it is a cleansing from all unrighteousness — "from the very principle that gives birth to sin."[89]

We can reach a point of maturity in the will of God where the Spirit of God perfects what he has already been developing. "Instead of remaining infants let us grow up in every respect" (Eph 4:14-15). "Let us go on unto maturity" (Heb 6:1). It is a mistake for people to claim this perfecting grace, however, when they barely have grasped what it means

---

[89]Pope, *PCNT*, 4:297.

to be justified by grace through faith.

Soon after conversion we realize that our sinful nature is not pleasing to God. He can give us victory. Part of that victory is self-control. However, we must not become proud of our efforts. No amount of discipline will make the sinful heart holy. "Having begun by the Spirit, are you now being perfected by the flesh?" (Gal 3:3) The victory is a cleansing promised from that nature.

According to Colossians 2:23 asceticism is of no value in stopping the indulgence of the flesh. *Asceticism* refers to the physical training of athletes and to the self-denial of the Stoics and Cynics. We cannot overcome temptation and guilt, addiction and compulsive behavior by human effort. Self-mortification or flagellation cannot drive out demons. Legalism is based on the false premise that we can save ourselves. According to Paul, this in fact is a form of worldliness. He mocks such extrabiblical rules in Colossians 2:21. Jesus directed his most angry words against the Pharisees (Matt 23). In contrast Wesley described the early Methodists,

> Nor do we desire to be distinguished by actions, customs, or usages of an indifferent nature. Our religion does not lie in doing what God has not enjoined or abstaining from what God has not forbidden.[90]

Within the holiness movement some have even become harsh and judgmental. Many testimonies center around what the person "had to do" rather than faith in what Jesus has done. This so-called "death route" sanctification.

Lillian Harvey and her family could not find a church

---

[90]Wesley, *BE Works*, 9:34.

which was spiritual enough to suit them. She believed that her sinful nature could be eradicated. However, she continued to feel sinful impulses. In her attempt to sanctify herself she jumped up and down on the side walk, praising God in public. Because she struggled to die to the flesh, she entered "five years of darkness" which was lifted only when she became willing to testify publically on a trolley bus. During that five-year period, she remained outwardly devout and was "living in hell." For the rest of her life, she believed that if she ever disobeyed God again she might revert back to this "hell."

This is a pathetic and pathological testimony of "Christless holiness." God gave us some inhibitions and it is not a sin to observe social conventions and etiquette. But the greatest distortion concerns the nature of God.[91] Wesley also made an important distinction between a Stoic and a Christian.[92]

In contrast Wesley wrote, "I believe this perfection is always wrought in the soul by a simple act of faith; consequently, in an instant. But I believe in a gradual work, both preceding and following that instant."[93] He preached

> Exactly as we are justified by faith, so are we sanctified by faith. Faith is the condition, and the only condition of sanctification, exactly as it is of justification. It is the condition: none is sanctified but he that believes; without faith no man is sanctified. And it is the only condition: this alone is sufficient for

---

[91]Tait, "Born in the Fire," 133-147.

[92]Wesley, *Letter* to Jane Catherine March, 30 Nov 1774.

[93]Wesley, *BE Works*, 13:199.

sanctification.[94]

That great truth, "that we are saved by faith," will never be worn out; and that sanctifying as well as justifying faith is the free gift of God. Now, with God one day is as a thousand years. It plainly follows that the quantity of time is nothing to him. Centuries, years, months, days, hours, and moments are exactly the same. Consequently, he can as well sanctify in a day after we are justified as an hundred years.[95]

Because this sanctifying grace is by faith and not by works it can happen in a moment and ought to be expected every moment. He wrote, "Strongly exhort all believers to expect full sanctification now by simple faith."[96]

Believe . . . that he is not only able, but willing to do it *now*! Not when you come to die; not at any distant time; not tomorrow, but *today*. He will then enable you to believe, *it is done*, according to his word.[97]

However, expecting this gracious gift any moment does not mean that we must first claim it in order to receive it. Phoebe Palmer advocated a naked trust in the naked Word of God. What Palmer called *faith*, Wesley would have called

---

[94]Wesley, "Scripture Way of Salvation," Sermon # 43, 3.3

[95]Wesley, *Letter* to Ann Foard, 12 Oct 1764.

[96]Wesley, *Letter* to John Ogilvie, 7 Aug 1785.

[97]Wesley, "On Patience," Sermon #83, § 13.

presumption.[98] The early Methodists were quick to seek sanctifying grace, but slow to profess it.[99] They did not claim it without the fruit. They did not wait passively, but continued to attend to all the means of grace.

Thus, we press forward with the divine conviction that God has promised complete cleansing from all sin. That he is able to perform what he has promised. We also have a divine conviction that he is able and willing to do it now.

> To this confidence that God is both able and willing to sanctify us *now*, there needs to be added one thing more — a divine evidence and conviction that *he doth it.* . . . Expect it *by faith*, expect it *as you are*, and expect it *now!*[100]

---

[98]See Reasoner, *Holy Living*, 544-562 for a more extensive evaluation of Palmer's theology.

[99]Tracy, "Entire Sanctification and Uncertain Trumpets," 6-7.

[100]Wesley, "The Scripture Way of Salvation," Sermon #43, 3.17-18.

Ninth Paper. The Full Assurance of Faith

The verb πληροφορέω (*plerophoreo*) is made up of two words: *full* and *to carry*. It means fully assured. One cannot be *fully* assured and doubt simultaneously.

Plerophoreo is used as a verb in Colossians 4:12 to describe the spiritual maturity of Epaphras. It is used as a noun in Colossians 2:2 where Paul expresses his desire that they might know the freedom of mind and confidence that comes from a full understanding of the mystery of God in Christ. This full assurance of understanding includes a systematic grasp of all the truths and treasures of the faith. In Wesley's words, "the fullest and clearest understanding and knowledge of the Gospel."[101] Clarke defined the full assurance of understanding as "the most indubitable certainty of the truth of Christianity, of their own salvation, and of the general design of God to admit the Gentiles into his Church."[102] Thus, this full assurance of understanding is an abiding and continual affirming by the Spirit of truth which produces a life of confidence.

Scripture also speaks of the full assurance of faith in 1 Thessalonians 1:5 and Hebrews 10:22. Wesley taught this full

---

[101]Wesley, *Notes*, 519.

[102]Clarke, *Commentary*, 6:521.

assurance of faith is "the common privilege of Christians."[103] According to Yates, "the full assurance of faith relates to present pardon; the full measure of hope, to future glory."[104] Wesley wrote,

> The plerophory (or full assurance) of faith is such a divine testimony that we are reconciled to God as excludes all doubt and fear concerning it. This refers only to what is present.[105]

Scripture even promises the full assurance of hope. The full assurance of hope in Hebrews 6:11 should be understood as an objective confidence based on the promises in God's Word regarding the success of Christ's kingdom. "And *perseverance* is nothing but the holding that *full assurance of hope unto the end.*"[106]

In the same letter to Elizabeth Ritchie, Wesley defined the full assurance of hope as "a direct testimony that we shall endure to the end; or, more directly, that we shall enjoy God in glory." I am not sure that this definition can be reconciled with the fact that all of life is a probationary period. Clarke cautioned that the full assurance of hope cannot imply that a man will absolutely persevere to the end since the Scripture does not teach unconditional perseverance.[107] Elsewhere,

---

[103]Wesley, *Letter* to Dr. Rutherforth, 28 March 1768.

[104]Yates, *The Doctrine of Assurance*, 128-132.

[105]Wesley, *Letter* to Elizabeth Ritchie, 6 Oct 1778.

[106]Pope, *Compendium*, 3:147.

[107]Clarke, *Commentary*, 6:727; see also Summers, *Systematic Theology*, 2:209-210; see my discussion in *Holy Living*, 1:295-302.

Wesley explained that "it does not, and cannot, continue any longer than we walk closely with God."[108] He also wrote, "And this confidence is totally different from an opinion that 'no saint shall fall from grace.' It has no relation to it."[109] Therefore, I am suggesting that it should be defined in a corporate sense — faith in the power of the gospel and faith in the final triumph of Christ's kingdom on earth.

According to Pope, the full assurance or *pleophory* of faith, of hope, and of understanding are three various forms of the same thing — the sure conviction of the reality of the object personally trusted in, hoped for, and apprehended in knowledge.[110]

If any distinction can be made, it seems that the full assurance of understanding refers to objective truth, the full assurance of faith refers to personal salvation, and the full assurance of hope describes a hope for the future. Perfect love always hopes (1 Cor 13:7).

In contrast to those who are ever learning but never able to come to a knowledge of the truth (2 Tim 3:7), assurance describes a spiritual maturity in which the believer lives in confidence of the truth. Paul said he was persuaded (πείθω - *peitho*; Rom 8:38, 14:14; 2 Tim 1:5) or fully convinced. John uses the verb εἰδέω (*eideo*) sixteen times and the verb (γινώσκω - *ginosko*) twenty-four times in 1 John. In this general letter John deals with objective knowledge and subjective assurance. The noun παρρησία (*parrhesia*), describing boldness and confidence, also occurs four times.

We do not have to be tossed back and forth with every

---

[108]Wesley, *Letter* to Philothea Briggs, 20 May 1771.

[109]Wesley, *Letter* to Hester Ann Roe, 10 April 1781.

[110]Pope, *Prayers of St. Paul*, 214.

new theological trend (Eph 4:14). We can know what we believe, and that belief can be rooted in a reality that corresponds with Scripture and produce a transformed life. We know God exists and his Word is true. We know we are forgiven and accepted. We know that we have been born again and that we have the Holy Spirit. We know that in the end truth will conquer.[111] Such assurance is based upon the Word of God and is made personal through the indwelling Holy Spirit.

---

[111]John Wyclif stated this belief [Schaff, *History of the Christian Church*, 6:320].

Tenth Paper. Faith for the Future

Jesus asked whether he would find faith on the earth when he returned (Luke 18:8). This question might imply a negative answer but we are also told that the gospel will go to all nations (Matt 24:14) and that all Israel shall be saved (Rom 11:26). Furthermore, Jesus taught us to pray that God's will would be done on earth as it is in heaven.

Therefore, Scripture provides a basis for hope that Christian faith will be flourishing when Christ returns. In fact, he will not return until every enemy is defeated (Ps 110:1). In context, the rhetorical question Jesus raised was not one of doubt. Rather, he was declaring that it would take the persistent faith that the widow exemplified in Luke 18:1-7 in order for the church to weather the storm. But such grace is available. Thus, Wesley anticipated a *"Christian world."* [112]

Ultimately, there will be people in heaven from every *nation, language,* and *ethnic group,* according to Revelation 5:9, 7:9, 10:11, 11:9, 13:7, 14:6, 17:15. This phrase is so significant that it also occurs six times in Daniel. It incorporates every political division, every linguistic barrier, and every cultural identity.[113] Yet everyone seen in heaven was saved on earth and the result is a host too great to count

---

[112]Wesley, "Scriptural Christianity," Sermon #4, 3.1.

[113]Reasoner, *Revelation*, 1:285-287.

(Rev 7:9). Therefore, Jesus was not asking whether or not Christianity would survive. He was asking each of us individually whether we had the faith to persevere.

All the ends of the world shall remember and turn unto the Lord, and all the families of the nations shall worship before you. All nations you have made shall come and worship before you, O Lord, and shall glorify thy name. It shall come to pass in the latter days that the mountain of the house of the Lord shall be established as the highest of the mountains, and shall be lifted up above the hills; and all nations shall flow unto it; and many peoples shall come and say: "Come, let us go up to the mountain of the Lord, to the house of the God of Jacob, that he may teach us his ways and we will walk in his paths." For out of Zion shall go forth the law, and the word of God from Jerusalem. And he will swallow up on this mountain the covering that is cast over all peoples, the veil that is spread over all nations. He will swallow up death forever, and the Lord God will wipe away tears from all faces; and the reproach of his people he will take away from all the earth, for the Lord has spoken. From new moon to new moon, and from one Sabbath to Sabbath, all flesh come to worship before me, declares the Lord. For the earth shall be filled with the knowledge of the glory of the Lord as the waters cover the sea. And no longer shall each one teach his neighbor and each his brother, saying, "Know the Lord," for they shall all know me, from the least of them to the greatest. He shall judge between the nations, and they shall beat their swords into plowshares, and their spears into pruning hooks; nation shall not lift up sword against nation, neither shall ye learn war any more. The wolf shall dwell with the lamb, and the leopard shall lie down with the young goat, and the calf and the lion and the fatted calf together; and a little child shall lead them. They shall not hurt or destroy in all my holy mountain. But they shall sit every man under his vine and under his fig tree, and no one shall make them afraid, for the mouth of the Lord of hosts has spoken. Go ye into all the world and proclaim the gospel to the whole creation. And this gospel of the kingdom will be proclaimed throughout the whole world as a testimony to all nations, and then the end will come. And I, when I am lifted up from the earth will draw all people to myself. Your kingdom come, your will be done, on earth as it is in heaven.[114]

As the old hymn says, "I dare not trust the sweetest frame [of mind], but wholly lean on Jesus' name." Our hope for the future is based on the following doctrines:

- God is sovereign and he will have the last word.
- Christ conquered Satan at the cross.
- The Holy Spirit has been poured out and he moves wherever he wills.
- The Bible is true and truth is stronger than error. Darkness cannot overcome the light (John 1:5).
- The gospel is the power of God and that confidence is not misplaced (Rom 1:16).
- The kingdom of Christ is predestined to cover the earth.

The victory of the cross is the *decisive* victory of Christ over Satan. The victory of the Christian church, through the atonement of Christ and enforced through our testimony, amounts to the *progressive* victory of Christ until his return. We live between those two great events. Satan has been in

---

[114]In this compilation, Raymond drew from Ps 22:27, 86:9; Isa 2:2-3, 25:7-8, 66:23; Hab 2:14; Jer 31:34; Isa 2:4, 11:6-9; Micah 4:4; Mark 16:15; Matt 24:14; John 12:32; Matt 6:10 [*Systematic Theology*, 2:474-476].

check mate since the cross.

Oscar Cullman developed the analogy of D-Day and V-Day to explain the decisive and the *final* victory of Christ. Based on World War 2 history, D-Day was the victory of the cross. However, the battle was not over at D-Day. Yet the second world war turned at D-Day from a defensive battle to an offensive battle — which culminated at V-Day.[115]The third and final defeat of Satan is described in Revelation 20:10. Until then, we can live in the victory already won at the cross.

---

[115]Ladd, *The Last Things*, 47.

Appendix A: THE FAITH FACTOR
Published in *The Arminian Magazine* 18:2 (Fall 2000) 1-3

If we are justified by faith, it should come as no surprise that the devil would attempt to redefine "faith." As this conference opens, I want to give an overview of our concerns. I am concerned that saving faith is being redefined in three major areas.

1. Saving faith is a present tense faith.

The Greek verb πιστεύω occurs 244 times in the New Testament. Many references in the Gospels and Acts are a matter of historical record. I am particularly interested in ninety usages which state general commands or promises.[116]

Participles

In each of the six instances of the aorist participle, the action of the participle occurs prior to the action of the main verb. In these instances they first believed and then received. However, none of these passages can be used to teach that a one-time act of faith is all that God requires.

There is one perfect participle used in Titus 3:8 and refers to action which has come to be a state of being.

---

[116]See Appendix B.

The present participle is used 48 times which denotes continuous action. This accounts for over half of all the usages we are considering.

The Imperative Mood

The imperative mood occurs in only two tenses - present tense and aorist tense. There is one aorist infinitive construction in Hebrews 11:6 which has the force of an imperative, but it refers to the initial act of coming to God. The other six times the imperative is present continuous action.

The Indicative Mood

The perfect tense indicates a past action with a continuing result. Certainly this emphasis is present in the five perfect indicatives which are used. The present indicative is used six times and indicates continuous action.

However, there are two aorist indicatives found. The use of the aorist in Galatians 2:16 refers to the crisis act of faith necessary in order that we might be justified. However, this verse could not be interpreted as meaning a single act of faith would guarantee final salvation. 1 Cor 15:2 refers to those who believed in vain.

The Subjunctive Mood

The subjunctive mood describes that which is potential. Often it carries the idea of *if*. Mildred Wynkoop observed that the Greek subjunctive indicates not only possibility, but also condition. It stands between predestination and moral choices.

It opens up possibility, but does not determine result.[117]

There are thirteen subjunctives and about an equal number of present subjunctives and aorist subjunctives. All refer to contingent action. Present subjunctives refer to continuous action while aorist subjunctives refer to a crisis act. None of the aorist subjunctives indicate that a crisis act will insure eternal salvation, but that a crisis act is necessary to be saved.

Romans 10:9 does uses an aorist subjunctive to refer to the crisis act of faith, but this promise is followed up in the next verse (v 10) with a present tense faith. "With the heart believe is exercised" (the only example of a passive voice).

While there are a few instances of commands which emphasize the crisis moment of faith, we can say that every stated promise of eternal life or eternal reward to those who believe is based on a present tense continuous faith.

It is ironic that the popular gospel teaching today proclaims that a sinner is free to choose or reject Christ, but once becoming a Christian he then loses the power of contrary choice. That momentary decision can never be reversed. This misconception is based upon a static and unscriptural understanding of faith. True faith is like breathing; we have to keep on.

Joseph Benson, an early Methodist commentator, preached on the text from 2 Peter 3:17-18, "Beware, lest ye also, being led away with the error of the wicked, fall from your own steadfastness. But grow in grace." The title of his message says it all, "Growth in Grace the Only Security Against Falling From It."[118]

---

[117]Wynkoop, *Foundations of Wesleyan-Arminian Theology*, 119-121.

[118]Benson, *Sermons and Plans of Sermons,* 7:230-232.

2. Saving faith produces good works.

James tells us that the demons have an intellectual faith. They believe that there is one God, yet this knowledge has not converted them. Therefore, James concludes that faith which does not produce works is a dead faith (2:18-26). There is a difference between a "decision for Christ" and saving faith; true faith includes repentance.

As we live by faith Romans 1:17 also teaches that we grow in faith. Saving faith produces the fruit of the Spirit (Gal 5:22-23).Those who are born again do not walk after the flesh, but after the Spirit (Rom 8:4).

However, if faith is reduced to a momentary decision and our theology teaches that once having made that decision we can never perish, what will we do with those who have made a profession of faith but exhibit no fruit?

Lewis Sperry Chafer wrote that a believer could be a new creation and yet remain a carnal Christian without any change in character. He stated that the carnal Christian is also characterized by a walk that is on the same plane as that of the natural man.[119]

When Chafer's book *He That Is Spiritual* was first published in 1918 it was extremely controversial. John MacArthur wrote, "Prior to this century, no serious theologian would have entertained the notion that it is possible to be saved yet see nothing of the outworking of regeneration in one's lifestyle or behavior." MacArthur went on to say that Chafer's concept of two classes of Christians, carnal and spiritual, "was a foreign concept to most Christians in Dr. Chafer's generation, but it has become a central premise for a large segment of the church today." It "became the basis for a

---

[119]Chafer, *He That Is Spiritual*, 12.

whole new way of looking at the gospel."[120]

Modern dispensationalists have carried their doctrine of the carnal Christian to such absurdities as claiming that you can't tell a carnal believer from a lost man because they both act the same way. This explains how Christians can steal, lie, commit adultery or suicide and still go to heaven. It has even been taught that a carnal Christian can fall away from the faith, cease believing, and still be eternally secure.[121]John MacArthur also documents the teaching of some that believers out of fellowship may be "unbelieving believers," even agnostics or atheists, yet even those who deny God are still eternally secure.[122]

Yet Romans 6 asserts that justification and initial sanctification are bound together and we cannot have the one without having the other. Randall Gleason wrote that Chafer over emphasized the discontinuity between justification and sanctification and underestimated the transforming power of regeneration. "To imagine that a person can be justified without any change for the better in his condition demonstrates a deficient view of both justification and sanctification."[123]

The term *old man* occurs three times in Paul's writings. In Romans 6:6 Paul states that our old man was crucified with Christ. Colossians 3:9 declares that believers have put off their old way of life. Ephesians 4:22 is an imperative for

---

[120]MacArthur, *The Gospel According to Jesus*, 23-25.

[121]Statements from Charles Stanley, Tony Evans, Chuck Swindoll, and others are compiled by Corner, *The Believer's Conditional Security*, 153-164.

[122]MacArthur, *The Gospel According to Jesus*, 98.

[123]Gleason, "B. B. Warfield and Lewis S. Chafer on Sanctification," 241-256.

Christians to put it off.[124] It is both an inconsistency to teach that one can become born again without any change and an inconsistency to teach that a believer can switch back and forth between the old lifestyle and the new.

Anthony Hoekema said the basic problem with the two natures position, as stated by John Walvoord, was that

> he fails to do full justice to the fact that a decisive break with sin was brought about by Christ for believers — so that sin, though still present in the believer, no longer has dominion — and to the amazing truth that the believer is now indeed, a new creature, old things having passed away. . . . He gives the impression that the Christian is something like a spiritual seesaw with two contradictory types of inner tendencies. With both tugging at one's heart, a believer can go either way.[125]

Therefore, we have today people who are making a mo-

---

[124]Bruce, *NICNT*, 357.

[125]Hoekema, "The Reformed View," 231. Shank asserts that the believer is a single spiritual entity and whatever he does, he does as a whole man [*Life in the Son*, 212-216]. John Murray wrote, "The believer is both old man and new man; when he does well he is acting in terms of the new man which he is; when he sins he is acting in terms of the old man which he also still is. This interpretation does not find support in Paul's teaching. . . . The old man is the unregenerate man; the new man is the regenerate man created in Christ Jesus unto good works. It is no more feasible to call the believer a new man and an old man, than it is to call him a regenerate man and an unregenerate. . . . Our old man has been crucified" [*Principles of Conduct*, 211-218].

mentary decision for Christ, who produce no evidence of salvation and yet are told daily by radio preachers that they cannot lose this salvation. But there are no unconditional covenants in Scripture.[126] While certain verses taken out of context may appear to offer unconditional security, they must be reconciled with the many conditions stated.

Furthermore, every passage which describes the final judgment states that we will be judged in that day on the basis of our works.[127] It is ironic that the sinner is held morally responsible to obey God, but when he becomes a Christian faithfulness is not required. The Christian, according to popular teaching, is judged at a lower standard.

3. Saving faith brings assurance.

The third deficiency in the false faith promoted today is that it produces no divine assurance. According to Hebrews 11:1, true faith produces assurance or confidence. This word υποστασις (*hupostasis*) was found in papyri sources to denote a title deed.[128] William Lane translates this opening phrase in

---

[126]see John Wesley, "Predestination Calmly Considered," *Works*,10:238-242; *BE Works*, 13:296-300; see also "Letter to a Gentleman at Bristol," *Works*, 10:308-310; *BE Works*, 13:361-363.

[127]Rom 14:10-12; 1 Cor 4:5; 2 Cor 5:10; Rev 20:12-13; Rev 22:12. If our works are imputed and not actual and if the basis of judgment is our works, then the nominal Christian would be condemned along with the sinner. To handle this dilemma dispensationalists have adopted a division of judgments with one for sinners on the basis of works and one for believers to determine the degree of reward. The Scriptures teach a general judgment.

[128]Moulton and Milligan, *Vocabulary of the Greek New Testament*, 659-660.

Hebrews 11:1, "Now faith celebrates the objective reality of the blessings for which we hope."[129]

Faith is also the evidence or proof of things not seen. John Wesley preached that

faith is a divine evidence and conviction, not only that "God was in Christ, reconciling the world unto himself," but also that Christ "loved *me* and gave himself for *me*." . . . And it is certain this faith necessarily implies an *assurance* . . . that "Christ loved *me*, and gave himself for *me*." For "he that believeth" with the true, living faith "hath the witness in himself." The Spirit witnesseth with his spirit that he is a child of God. Because he is a son, God hath sent forth the Spirit of His Son into his heart, crying, Abba, Father; giving him an assurance that he is so, and a childlike confidence in him.[130]

A false faith produces no assurance. However, the Holy Spirit still convicts of sin (John 16:8). This conviction creates anxiety and secular psychology complains that religion upsets people.

Recently a psychiatrist told a woman who had attended our services that she was too religious. She was so upset by his advice that she quit him and started back to church. The Lord has helped her greatly.

But the "carnal Christian" should be upset. Ten percent of the total Christian population is sexually addicted.[131] The

---

[129]Lane, *WBC*, 47B:325.

[130]Wesley, "The Scripture Way of Salvation," Sermon #43, 2.3.

[131]Laaser, *The Secret Sin*, 15.

"carnal Christian" should be anxious because the Scripture teaches that sexual immorality, impurity and debauchery; idolatry and witchcraft; hatred, discord, jealousy, fits of rage, selfish ambition, dissension, factions and envy; drunkenness, orgies, and the like are acts of the sinful nature and those who live like this will not inherit the kingdom of God (Gal 5:19-21).

So, the Holy Spirit convicts, but he is not bringing assurance to the "carnal Christian." The right kind of preaching would produce more conviction! The popular preachers teach a false assurance based on their rationalistic doctrine of "once saved, always saved." They teach I can have it and not feel it, but I can never lose it if I ever get it! I would rather know that I am saved and yet know that salvation could be forfeited than to be talked into a profession that I did not possess, but told I could not lose.

While the Holy Spirit convicts the nominal Christian that they are not ready to meet God, these preachers misapply the Word of God by teaching a false security while the Holy Spirit calls for surrender. Yet the logic of their teaching cannot compete with the gentle whisper of the Holy Spirit. The mind of the nominal Christian may accept the logic of the smooth teacher, but in his heart he knows something is not right.

Let me offer some sound psychological advice. Quit trying to justify what God's Word condemns. Agree with the voice of the Holy Spirit and surrender to the lordship of Christ. God will then enable you to believe and when you trust in Christ with all your heart, He will come through His Spirit and make a new person out of you. You will know that you are truly saved because the Holy Spirit will bring peace and because you see the indirect evidence of a changed life.

But some might object that this Wesleyan-Arminian

emphasis is conditional. This salvation may be forfeited. Apostasy is a real possibility. They often scoff that we have no assurance. They caricature us as believing that "every *other* day with Jesus is sweeter than the day before." That we have be born again and again and again. On the other hand, they are eternally secure.

I am arguing that we offer more actual security than they do. John Wesley did preach that salvation is conditional. But he also preached

> that the Spirit of God does give a believer such a testimony of his adoption that *while it is present to the soul* he can no more doubt the reality of his sonship than he can doubt of the shining of the sun while he stands full blaze of his beams.[132]

A present tense faith produces a present tense assurance.

We protest this false faith which does not require any commitment or obedience beyond an initial decision. It is a dead faith which produces no spiritual fruit and brings no divine assurance. If a church member exercises no faith, gives no evidence of having been saved, and has no supernatural assurance that he is saved — it should be obvious that he is not saved!

Before the modern teaching of the dispensationalists confused the issue, in little towns and villages across this nation there was a time when the Baptists had revival and the Methodists would join them. When the Methodists had their camp meeting the Baptists came. If the Presbyterians scheduled a protracted meeting, the other denominations came to

---

[132]Wesley, "The Witness of the Spirit, I," Sermon #10, 1.12. Italics added.

fellowship. But if a seeker came forward, it did not matter which denominational he preferred, it was expected that when he really got saved there would be a change in his life. Yes, there were differences between the denominations. They had different traditions and there were variations in their rituals of worship, but they all believed that salvation did something for a man. If a man or woman professed to get religion and their life did not change, it was generally agreed that the religion did not "take."

We preach a free gospel for all men and a full gospel from all sin. It is based upon a present tense faith which produces good works and brings assurance. We believe that if we keep ourselves in the love of God he is able to keep us from falling (Jude 21-24) and that he will appear a second time to bring final salvation to those who are believing (Heb 9:28). This is the faith which saves.

APPENDIX B. A Concordance of Πιστεύω

This list represents the ninety general uses of the verb *believe* in the New Testament. Each instance is parsed with regard to tense, voice, and mood. Tense indicates the time and kind of action. Voice is either active or passive. Mood indicates the relationship of the verb to reality. Participles are translated in relationship to the main verb. See detailed explanation on pp. 68-70.

Mark 1:15 repent and believe - present active imperative
John 1.7 aorist active subjunctive
1:12 present active participle
3:15-16 present active participles
18 twice present active participles; last occurrence perfect active indicative
36 present active participle
5:24 present active participle
6:29 present active subjunctive
35 present active participle
40 present active participle
47 present active participle
7:38 present active participle
39 aorist active participle - those who believed would receive the Spirit
8:24 aorist active subjunctive
10:38 present active subjunctive

11:25 present active participle
26 present active participle; present active indicative
42 aorist active subjunctive
12:36 present active imperative
44 present active participle
46 present active participle
13:19 present active subjunctive
14:1 both present active imperatives (first could be indicative)
11 both present active imperatives
12 present active participle
29 aorist active subjunctive
16:27 perfect active indicative
31 present active indicative
17:20 present active participle
21 present active subjunctive
19:35 present active subjunctive
20:29 perfect active indicative; aorist active participle - not yet seeing, yet believed prior to sight
31 present active subjunctive; present active participle
Acts 10:43 present active participle
13:39 present active participle
16:31 aorist active imperative
19:4 aorist active subjunctive
Rom 1:16 present active participle
3:22 present active participle
4:5 present active participle
11 present active participle
24 present active participle
9:33 present active participle
10:4 present active participle
9 aorist active subjunctive
10 present passive indicative

11 present active participle
15:13 present active infinitive - the use of the article makes
  it function as a participle
1 Cor 1:21 present active participle
13:7 present active indicative
14:22 both present active participles
15:2 aorist active indicative - in vain
Gal 2:16 aorist active indicative
3:22 present active participle
Eph 1:13 aorist active participle - the faith was prior to the
  sealing
19 present active participle
Phil 1:29 present active infinitive - with article; functions as
  a participle
1 Thess 2:10 present active participle
13 present active participle
4:14 present active indicative
2 Thess 1.10 aorist active participle - believed prior to a
  future event
2:12 aorist active participle - believed prior to a future event
1 Tim 1:16 present active infinitive - with article functions as
  a participle
2 Tim 1:12 perfective active indicative
Titus 3:8 perfect active participle
Heb 4:3 aorist active participle - believed prior to entering
  rest
11:6 aorist infinitive - the force of an imperative
James 2:19 both present active indicatives
1 Peter 1:8 present active participle
21 present active participle
2:6 present active participle
7 present active participle
1 John 3:23 aorist active subjunctive - a crisis act

4:16 perfect active indicative
5:1 present active participle
5 present active participle
10 first two - present active participles; perfect active indicative
13 present active participle

BIBLIOGRAPHY

Arminius, James. *The Works of James Arminius*. 3 vols. The London Edition. 1825-1875. Reprint, Grand Rapids: Baker, 1996.

Arndt, William F. and F. Wilbur Gingrich. *A Greek-English Lexicon of the New Testament*. 2nd ed. Chicago: University of Chicago Press, 1979.

Augustine. *Homilies on the Gospels. A Select Library of the Nicene and Post-Nicene Fathers of the Christian Church.* First Series. Vol. 6. Philip Schaff, ed. 1887. Reprint, Grand Rapids. Eerdmans, 1979. [*NPNF*]

Bebbington, David W. *The Dominance of Evangelicalism*. Vol. 3 of *A History of Evangelicalism*. Downers Grove, IL: InterVarsity, 2005.

Benson, Joseph. *Sermons and Plans of Sermons*. 7 vols. Baltimore: Armstrong & Plaskitt, 1828. 7:230-232. Sermon #251.

Binney, Amos and Daniel Steele. *The People's Commentary on the New Testament*. New York: Eaton & Mains, 1878.

Bloesch, Donald G. *Faith and Its Counterfeits*. Downers Grove, IL: InterVarsity, 1981.

Bonhoeffer, Dietrich. *The Cost of Discipleship*. 2nd ed. R. H. Fuller, transl. New York: Macmillan, 1960.

Bruce, F. F. *The Epistles to the Colossians, to Philemon, and to the Ephesians: The New International Commentary on the New Testament*. Grand Rapids: Eerdmans, 1984.

[*NICNT*]

Bunting, Jabez. *Justification by Faith. A Sermon Preached in Albion-Street Chapel, at Leeds, On Monday, July Twenty-seventh, 1812 and Published at the Request of the Methodist Conference, Then assembled in that Town.* 2nd ed. Leeds: James Nichols, 1814.

Burwash, Nathaniel, ed. *Wesley's Doctrinal Standards.* Toronto: William Briggs, 1881.

Capps, Charles. *Releasing the Ability of God Through Prayer.* Broken Arrow, OK: Capps Publishing, 2004.

_____. *The Tongue: A Creative Force.* Broken Arrow, OK: Capps Publishing, 1976.

Chafer, Lewis Sperry. *He That Is Spiritual.* 1918. Reprinted, Philadelphia: Sunday School Times, 1924.

Clarke, Adam. *The Holy Bible, Containing the Old and New Testaments: The Text Carefully Printed from the Most Correct Copies of the Present Authorized Translations, Including the Marginal reading and Parallel Tests; with a Commentary and Critical Notes, Designed as a help to a Better Understanding of the Sacred Writings.* 6 vols. 1811-1825. Reprint, Nashville: Abingdon, 1950.

Comfort, Ray and Kirk Cameron. *The School Of Biblical Evangelism.* Gainsville, FL: Bridge-Logos, 2004.

Copeland, Kenneth. *Our Covenant with God.* Ft. Worth, TX: Kenneth Copeland Publications, 1976.

_____. *Freedom from Fear.* Ft. Worth, TX: Kenneth Copeland Publications, 1980.

_____. *The Force of Faith.* Ft. Worth, TX: Kenneth Copeland Publications, 1983.

Corner, Daniel D. *The Believer's Conditional Security.* Washington, PA: Evangelical Outreach, 1997.

Farah, Charles. *From the Pinnacle of the Temple.* Plainfield, NJ: Logos, 1978.

Fletcher, John. *The Works of the Reverend John Fletcher.* 1833. Reprint, Salem, OH: Schmul, 1974.

Forlines, F. Leroy. "Election in Romans 9: Conditional or Unconditional?" Evangelical Theological Society Papers, Southeastern Regional Conference, March 4-5, 1998, Chattanooga, TN.

Foster, Randolf S. *Philosophy of Christian Experience.* New York: Hunt & Eaton, 1890.

Gleason, Randall. "B. B. Warfield and Lewis S. Chafer on Sanctification," *Journal of the Evangelical Theological Society* 40:2 (June 1997) 241-256.

Hagin, Kenneth E. *New Thresholds in Faith.* Tulsa, OK: Kenneth Hagin Ministries, 1980.

_____. *Bible Faith Study Course.* Tulsa: Faith Library, 1981.

Hamilton, Victor P. *Handbook on the Pentateuch.* 2nd ed. Grand Rapids: Baker, 2005.

Hanegraff, Hank. *Christianity in Crisis: 21st Century.* Nashville: Thomas Nelson, 2009.

Hinn, Costi W. *God, Greed and the Prosperity Gospel.* Grand Rapids: Zondervan, 2019.

Hoekema, Anthony A. "The Reformed View." *Five Views of Sanctification.* Grand Rapids: Zondervan, 1987.

Hollinger, Dennis. "Enjoying God Forever." *The Gospel and Contemporary Perspectives.* 2 vols. Douglas J. Moo, ed. Grand Rapids: Kregel, 1997.

Kaiser, Walter C. Jr. "The Old Testament Promise of Material Blessings and the Contemporary Believer." *Trinity Journal* 9:2 (Fall 1988) 151-170.

Keen, Samuel Ashton. *Faith Papers: A Treatise on Experimental Aspects of Faith.* Cincinnati: Cranston & Stowe, 1891.

Kenyon, Essek William. *The Hidden Man: An Unveiling of*

the Subconscious Mind. Seattle: Kenyon's Gospel Publishing, 1970.

Laaser, Mark R. *The Secret Sin.* Grand Rapids: Zondervan, 1992.

Ladd, George Eldon. *The Last Things.* Grand Rapids: Eerdmans, 1978.

Lane, William L. *Word Biblical Commentary: Hebrews 9-13.* Volume 47B. Dallas, Word, 1991.

Lewis, C. S. *The Problem of Pain.* New York: MacMillan, 1962.

Liardon, Roberts. *God's Generals.* Tulsa: Albury, 1996.

Lovett, C. S. "The Medicine of Your Mind." *Personal Christianity Newsletter* (Aug 1979).

Luther, Martin. *Luther's Works.* American ed. 79 vols. Javoslav Pelikam and Helmut T. Lehmann, eds. St. Louis: Concordia, 1955-2016.

MacArthur, John F. Jr. *The Gospel According to Jesus.* Grand Rapids: Zondervan, 1988.

McCain, Danny. "Prosperity: A Biblical Perspective." *African Journal of Biblical Studies* 15:2 (October 2000) 60-76.

McConnell, D. R. *A Different Gospel.* Peabody, MA: Hendrickson, 1988.

McIntyre, Patrick. *The Graham Formula.* Mammoth Spring, AR: White Harvest, 2006.

Moo, Douglas. *The Wycliffe Exegetical Commentary: Romans 1-8.* Kenneth Barker, ed. Chicago: Moody, 1991.

Moulton, J. H. and George Milligan. *Vocabulary of the Greek New Testament, Illustrated from the Papyri and Other Non-literary Sources.* Grand Rapids: Eerdmans, 1949.

Murray, John. *Principles of Conduct.* Grand Rapids: Eerdmans, 1957.

Oden, Thomas C. ed. "Phoebe Palmer as the Missing Link

Between Methodist and Pentecostal Spirituality." *Phoebe Palmer: Selected Writings*. New York: Paulist, 1988.

Palmer, Phoebe. *Faith and Its Effects: Fragments from my Portfolio*. 1848. Reprint, Salem, OH: Schmul, 1999.

Pivec, Holly and R. Doughlas Geivett. *Counterfeit Kingdom*. Nashville: B&H, 2022.

Pope, William Burt. *A Compendium of Christian Theology*. 3 vols. London: Wesleyan Conference Office, 1880.

_____. *A Higher Catechism of Theology*. London: T. Woolmer, 1885.

_____. *The Prayers of St. Paul*. 2nd ed. London: Charles H. Kelley, 1896.

_____. *I, II, II John: A Popular Commentary on the New Testament*. Philip Schaff, ed. Vol. 4. Edinburgh: T&T Clark, 1883 [*PCNT*]

Raymond, Miner. *Systematic Theology*. 3 vols. Cincinnati: Cranston & Stowe, 1877-1879.

Reasoner, Vic. "Justification: Imputed *and* Imparted: A Survey of Romans." Atlanta: Evangelical Theological Society, 17 November 2010. Unpublished.

_____. *A Wesleyan Theology of Holy Living for the Twenty-First Century*. 2 vols. Evansville, IN: Fundamental Wesleyan, 2012.

Roberts, Oral. *God Is a Good God: Believe It and Come Alive*. Indianapolis: Bobbs-Merrill, 1960.

_____. *If You Need Healing Do These Things*. Tulsa: Oral Roberts Evangelistic Association, 1947.

_____. *Daily Guide to Miracles and Successful Living Through Seed-Faith*. Tulsa: Pinoak, 1976.

Sarles, Ken L. "A Theological Evaluation of the Prosperity Gospel." *Bibliotheca Sacra* 143 (Oct/Nov 1986) 329-352.

Schaeffer, Francis. *The God Who Is There*. Downers Grove,

IL: InterVarsity, 1968.

_____. *The Finished Work of Christ: The Truth of Romans 1-8*. Westchester, IL: Crossway, 1998.

Schaff, Philip. *History of the Christian Church*. 8 vols. 5th ed. 1889. Reprint, Grand Rapids: Eerdmans, 1980.

Shank, Robert. *Life in the Son*. Springfield, MO: Westcott, 1961.

Smith, A. J. *Jesus Lifting Chinese*. 1928. Reprint, Salem, OH: Allegheny, 2007.

Smith, Timothy L. *Revivalism and Social Reform*. Baltimore: Johns Hopkins, 1980.

Steele, Daniel. *Half-Hours with St. Paul*. 1894. Reprint, Rochester, PA: Schmul, 1959.

_____. *Mile-Stone Papers*. 1878. Reprint, Salem, OH: Schmul, 1976.

Stevens, Abel. *Life and Times of Nathan Bangs, D. D.* New York: Carlton & Porter, 1863.

Summers, Thomas O. *Systematic Theology*. 2 vols. John Tigert, ed. Nashville: Methodist Episcopal Church, South, 1888.

Sutcliffe, Joseph. *A Commentary on the Old and New Testament*. 2 vols. 1834. Reprint, Salem, OH: Allegheny, 2000.

Synan. Vincent. "The Faith of Kenneth Hagin." *Charisma and Christian Life* 15:11 (June 1990) 63-70.

Tait, Edwin Woodruff. "Born in the Fire." *The Radical Holiness Movement in the Christian Tradition*. William Kostlevy and Wallace Thornton, Jr. eds. Lexington, KY: Emeth, 2016.

Tracy, Wesley. "Entire Sanctification and Uncertain Trumpets." *Herald of Holiness* 79:10 (October 1990) 6-7.

Tyerman, Luke. *The Life and Times of John Wesley*. 3 vols. London: Hodder & Stoughton, 1872.

Vine, W. E. *An Expository Dictionary of New Testament Words*. 4 vols in one. Old Tappan, NJ: Fleming H. Revell, 1952.

Waltke, Bruce K. *The Book of Proverbs 15-31: The New International Commentary on the Old Testament*. Grand Rapids: Eerdmans, 2005.

Wallace, Daniel B. *Gree Grammar Beyond the Basics*. Grand Rapids: Zondervan, 1996.

Watson, Richard. *A Biblical and Theological Dictionary*. New York: Carlton & Porter, 1832.

_____. *An Exposition of the Gospels of St. Matthew and St. Mark*. London: Wesleyan Conference Office, 1833.

Wesley, John. *The Bicentennial Edition of the Works of John Wesley*. 35 vols. when complete. Randy Maddox, ed. Nashville: Abingdon, 1975-. [*BE*]

_____. *Explanatory Notes Upon the New Testament*. 1754. Reprint, Salem, OH: Schmul, 1976.

Winter, Ralph D. "A Theology of Redemption, Part IV." *Mission Frontiers* 8:5 (May 1986) 15.

Wynkoop, Mildred. *Foundations of Wesleyan-Arminian Theology*. Kansas City: Beacon Hill, 1967.

Yates, Arthur S. *The Doctrine of Assurance*. London: Epworth, 1952.

www.ingramcontent.com/pod-product-compliance
Lightning Source LLC
Chambersburg PA
CBHW060345050426
42449CB00011B/2845